William E. F Krause

The German-French War of 1870 and Its Consequences upon Future Civilization

William E. F Krause

The German-French War of 1870 and Its Consequences upon Future Civilization

ISBN/EAN: 9783743383333

Manufactured in Europe, USA, Canada, Australia, Japa

Cover: Foto ©Suzi / pixelio.de

Manufactured and distributed by brebook publishing software (www.brebook.com)

William E. F Krause

The German-French War of 1870 and Its Consequences upon Future Civilization

GERMAN-FRENCH WAR OF 1870

AND

ITS CONSEQUENCES

UPON

FUTURE CIVILIZATION.

BY WM. E. F. KRAUSE,

AUTHOR OF "AMERICAN INTERESTS IN BORNEO," THE UNITED STATES INTERESTS ABROAD," AND A NUMBER OF POEMS IN THE ENGLISH AND GERMAN LANGUAGES.

SAN FRANCISCO, CAL.
JOS. WINTERBURN & COMPANY, PRINTERS AND ELECTROTYPERS,
No. 417 Clay Street, between Sansome and Battery.
1 8 7 2.

Rooms of the

ODD FELLOWS' LIBRARY ASSOCIATION.

SAN FRANCISCO, FEBRUARY 28th, 1872.

SIR:

I am requested by the Government of the Association to acknowledge your donation of your works on "BORNEO," "THE INFLUENCE OF THE UNITED STATES ABROAD," "AMERICA, THE HOPE OF MANKIND," "FOUR POEMS," "THE SANCTITY OF MARRIAGE," "22 POEMS IN THE GERMAN LANGUAGE," and the "HISTORY OF THE FRANCO-GERMAN WAR OF 1870," all of which have been bound and placed on our shelves, and to return their thanks for the same.

HENRY C. SQUIRE,
SECRETARY.

To W. E. F. KRAUSE, ESQ.
SAN FRANCISCO,
CALIFORNIA.

The anniversary of Mr. Krause's 20 years' residence in California. Arrival of the Steamship *Golden Gate*, Capt. Patterson, from Panama.

Entered according to act of Congress in the year 1872,
BY WM. E. F. KRAUSE,
In the Office of the Librarian of Congress, at Washington.

INDEX.

		PAGES.
PART I.	INTRODUCTORY: The Advance of Republicanism	1–11
	The War.	
	a. The Diplomacy of France and Prussia	11–21
	b. The Crown of Spain as proffered to the Prince of Hohenzollern Sigmaringen	21–28
	c. The acceptance of said Crown by a Prince of Hohenzollern considered by the government of Napoleon as a *casus belli*	28–34
PART II.	Napoleon's calculations of success in a war with Prussia, and the Declaration of War.	
	a. Napoleon's Calculations	34–37
	b. The non-interference by all the European nations	37–46
	c. The Official Declaration of War by France to Prussia	46–47
	d. Interesting Speeches and Diplomatic Correspondence between France and Prussia on the Subject of the Balance of Power in Europe	47–69
PART III.	The Provisional Battle Ground	69–72
PART IV.	The Prussian and French Army Organizations	72–78
PART V.	The War in Detail:	
	a. The Staff of Generals of the French and German Armies—The Executive Command over the entire German Army entrusted by the King of Prussia to General Moltke	78–79
	b. The Commencement of Hostilities	79–80
	c. The Battles...... 80–85. Continued from 100–112	
PART VI.	The French Republic	85–94
PART VII.	Why Peace was not concluded at Sedan	94–100
PART VIII.	The Capitulation of Strasburg and Metz—Naval Engagements	100–103

			PAGES.
PART	IX.	The Siege of Paris and the Battles against the Army of the Loire	103–112
PART	X.	The Consequences of the War upon Future Civilization	112–121
PART	XI.	Peace—The New Boundary of Germany	121–124
		a. The Preliminaries of Peace	124–129
PART	XII.	Germany at Home	129–134
PART	XIII.	Historical Future — The Regeneration of the Netherlands	134–139
PART	XIV.	The Cosmopolitan Power of the United States of America, Great Britain, and United Germany	139–142

SAN FRANCISCO, Cal., February 22d, 1872.

ERRATA.

Page 2, line 29th, read 1,000,000,000, instead of 1,000,000.
Page 40, line 15th, read *Tartary*, instead of Turkey.
Page 94, line 26th, read *the*, instead of they.
Page 95, line 34th, read *herself*, instead of itself.
Page 130, line 1st, read *welded*, instead of smelted.
Page 130, line 33d, read *civilized*, instead of barbarous.
Page 135, line 27th, read *her*, instead of its.
Page 135, line 30th, read *their*, instead of her.
Page 136, line 13th, read *best*, instead of but.
Page 141, line 15th, read *upon*, instead of to.

PART THE FIRST.

THE ADVANCE OF REPUBLICANISM.

It being an avowed characteristic of the high order of civilization attained to at this period of the world's history, for man and nations to sympathize with and aid in ameliorating the misfortunes of one another, it is quite natural that, we find the people of the United States not only averse to and regretting all wars, from principle, themselves politically acting upon its high commands, but observe them aggrieved at the war which in turn has devastated France, as affecting one of the most civilized nations by retarding its general progress of prosperity.

Truly loyal in their wishes for the maintenance of the Republic in France, and eager in discerning symptoms of a like improvement upon government in other civilized nations, the American people, while pondering over the extraordinary commotion of this war, experience a relief in the contemplation that with the tranquil demise of the venerable Emperor of Germany, the great intellectual union of the German people may signify the unveiling of the bright Goddess of Liberty in Germany, and, resting at her heart, feel its throbbings a mother's love for every child alike.

Then, with Great Britain and her colonies simultaneously to follow, there is indeed a fair prospect, at this age, for all mankind to become free! And how unlike the dark periods of history when the Romans failed in the permanency of the Republic through want of universal education, precluding a high state of morality, and were not guided to happiness by experience in the inestimable advantages of an enlightening Christianity.

With us the republican *versus* the monarchical government has stood a centennial test—enough positive proof of not only its rational superiority over all other forms of government, but of its admirable efficiency, *de facto*, and its indivisibility and feasibility in enlightened ages. It now excels as the most glorious achievement of progress, because under it can be, and with us has been, is daily, and shall forever be attained, the true object of all civilization; *the individ-*

ual *happiness of man to an universal extent*, duly commensurate with a steady advance in the general progress of civilization, so as to justify, as in accord with it, the prediction of its ultimate adoption by all nations, and to be by them regarded as manifest destiny, so soon as sufficiently enlightened and consequently unanimously determined of proclaiming, appreciating and revering it.

Its legitimacy is found sacred, inasmuch as all truth and knowledge is derived from an incessant and correct interpretation and judicious application of nature, which wisdom, by labor attained, as rendering man good, virtuous and prosperous, enables him to properly appreciate life, directing reason to guide him to actions which, when sagaciously applied to the present, create his happiness, and, united with others, expand civilization, in chronological order of the day, through all ages of time. So the earnest reflectant not merely perceives man as living in great numbers, scattered all over the earth, and originally born in mental and physical equality, but observes him as with impartiality tenderly cradled amidst the grand loveliness of nature, which, heralding the voice of God, distinguishes him as His image by the exuberance of his reasoning powers, and vouchsafes him happiness everywhere, while it demands of him the sacred duty of fraternity. This duty, be it understood, the American people, as a nation, really and almost only religiously obey, but which ought in this age to serve every civilized being as the syntax of the great study of the use of life, as acknowledged and demonstrated by civilization, which study is made altogether supreme in importance by the force of reflection upon the surety, as well as the mysterious uncertainty of the time, of death.

The duty of fraternity is realized from the fact of the existence at our age of about 1,000,000 people. Furthermore, God creating man and not nations, land and not countries, nature not only points to man's independence through his individuality, as an inalienable right wherever he lives, but to freedom of his actions and the liberty of his will. As man at all arrives at civilization through external influences, elevating his mind and cultivating his heart, so the circle of his personal friends shall widen in proportion of his own advance to that of others in usefulness and sympathetic attractiveness through education, refinement and social intercourse. Consequently, the more readily and generally the duty of fraternity is fulfilled, the more tolerant, forbearing and compassionate man is, the more communicative of his knowledge, the more considerate in his regard for the feelings of others, the more gracefully and unassumingly he deports himself—the more genteel and accomplished he is, the happier his life, the more religiously and sensibly does he act; and the more universal such enlightenment in a nation, the more civilized a people composed of such ladies and gentlemen, and the more conspicuous the truth of republicanism, which alone guarantees the independence of man.

Therefore no system of government is compatible with civilization in the fullest sense of the word, in which man, its first principle, its true idiom and object, is precluded from, is not considered morally fit for self-government; who, possessing the attribute of moral fitness, as emerged from cannibalism and heathenism, and with reasoning powers unimpaired, has unquestionably the right, from the fact that he adds at least some share of usefulness to the common wealth, of demanding participation in a government which consolidates but for the one object, and, unitedly only, successfully carries it out: the ennobling of man— the happiness and usefulness of all in the presence of God.

In order that all mankind may adopt our precedent, we, finding at least the European nations abundantly prepared for self-government, which is daily ascertained from the German and French as well as any other immigrant to whom we grant the vote and whom we receive into the bosom of our commonwealth with the kindness and trust of a friend—consequently whose brother (unfortunately for us left behind) is equally fit for voting there—it becomes not only necessary but a duty incumbent on the American people, as the most happy portion of the fraternity of mankind, of illustrating by all manner of means the direct effect of our institutions upon the happiness of men residing here and forming the American nation, to all foreigners outside, for their special edification and encouragement.

This duty effectually to carry out, which obviously is of such inestimable æsthetic worth to civilization, appears and becomes imperative from the standpoint of our institutions, by which we foster, a care for the interest of humanity in all places and at all times; while officially their peaceable tenor prescribes observance of strict neutrality in all international affairs. It includes the hope for an universal law ere long to be agreed upon and passed, by which wars may henceforth be peremptorily avoided through mutual obligations of settling all untowardly arising political dissensions by arbitration — substituting for expensive standing armies the economical volunteer system and similarly humane, rational and judicious derivations.

As an agreeable task, cheerfully undertaken, it is satisfactorily accomplished by manfully expressing our gratitude for the happiness we as a nation enjoy under the banner of freedom in this country, on all occasions, publicly and privately—availing ourselves especially of every foreign imbroglio to do so.

Such a feature would undoubtedly show its efficiency abroad because of its lawfulness and access to the censors. It convinces. To vituperatively denounce monarchical governments, or to praise our own in a pompous manner, could not be thought of an instant; both attempts at making the desired impression would prove altogether futile—the former with the ignorant abroad creating hatred, and with the powful a scornful delight; while the latter would present the American citizen altogether in a wrong light, likewise falling short of effect.

No; if the truth must be told, let every one prove his words by his residence in this country, and not for whole years in European capitals; by his quiet contentedness here, so envied by the wealthiest roaming cosmopolite; by his studied silence of opinion in regard to wars as unelating and disagreeably obvious of misery; by a profound disregard of the hollowness of a mere and altogether unreputed appearance of man, as best stifling in the bud the spirit of aristocratic intolerance; by a liberal acknowledgement of talent here and abroad; by lavish exhibitions of industry in this country, while promptly frequenting those of Europe; and by the diminution in the cost of steamship travel and of letter postage, viewed as the carriers of civilization, which make known to the world the truth of republics and influence emigration; and we cannot fail in drawing the attention of all foreign people upon us, touch with dignity and due effect the pernicious pride of the aristocrat, the obstinate enemy of fraternity and good will toward all men—the stoic skeptic in the religious truth of the republic — and we shall succeed in arousing an earnest longing and a fluttering among all classes to either emigrate here or to be similarly free and happy there, leaving man's opinion to mature on the spot, from the richness of facts received in double-quick time.

These facts, vividly illustrated, as they shall depict life in the United States in all phases of a veritably unsurpassed progress in civilization, the cause of freedom, of man's personal independence in this country; and of all the appliances of civilized life—free schools, a free press and free labor—and not of favorable natural advantages and a thinly-populated country only, so often, with lamentable ignorance, held forth as an argument by men, strange to say, in our very midst: these proofs are daily abundantly given, and are hourly carried by telegraph and by steam, in person, to and fro, the world over; in books and in letters, by millions; are magnificently displayed by the fabulous wealth of our commerce at home and abroad; then again, by the unknown existence at any time of a poverty-stricken multitude in our large cities, as one of the greatest blessings which republics only afford, where men are sworn by the vote to the duty of ameliorating the condition of one another, in order that all be drawn to the surface of ease and comfort, and no partiality shown in detriment to the divine rights of another, while purposely remiss in adulation of the wealth of the man whose individual usefulness to the country at large does not stand in exact proportion to it, or whose moral example is none, nor his heart known to pulsate audibly for love as well as public charities, as in the case of a charitable bachelor millionaire acquiring with enormous wealth the peculiar duty of judiciously disposing of the greater part of it to the public before he dies; by the etiquette of our National Government, which expects of the best of men as well as the most useful and learned to say to himself, "There are others aspiring to what I once honorably craved and now glory in, of having successfully attained"; by the less than nominal expense to the wealthiest nation upon earth of the care for the bodily comfort of the inmates of the White House, as in concert with the habits of the real American, who values wealth but as a medium of carrying out intelligent ideas—worthless to him as a clap-trap for either power, glory or fashion; and rising as another brilliant star to outshine the allurements of Europe, where the retinue of courts serves as a gas by which the fashionable avenues of trade are lit up; then, again, by the innumerable institutions of benevolence; by the respect and courtesy shown to every lady in every station of life; by the protection given and license of freedom granted to every child; and, above all, by the Press, in the light of a daily producer and conveyancer of wholesome as well as delicious nutriment for the mind of man, serving, caring and ambulancing the wounded hearts of mankind, without intermission, to the glory of civilization, besides being the most irrepressible arm of Freedom, the ever invulnerable shield of Liberty.

By such means as those enumerated, which we know are in constant, active use, and always on the increase ever since the telegraph and steam—in reality the manual hands of civilization,—have almost annihilated geographical distances, it appears an utter impossibility for the leading European nations to adhere any longer to monarchical governments and classifications of society which are not only unnatural but superannuated by the force of universal enlightenment. As a standard truth, this assertion is verified by the full weight of the naturalization oath resting upon it which the intelligent foreigner takes in this country when, from conviction and sheer intelligence, he abjures all allegiance to royalty as inconsistent with his conception of what is humanly right. In doing so he likewise abjures all sympathy with the usurped power of its mandates and adopts this country as his only home, because of its entire freedom from arbitrary and hereditary individual power, and with institutions drafted to that effect, as affording him the desired and expected guarantee for, and a permanent and peaceable enjoyment of, all his own individual and lawful rights.

In order to produce in California, or America generally, a synoptical portraiture sufficiently explanatory of the various causes which led to this memorable war, is perhaps preferably done by translating from some work, well spoken of on the continent of Europe, instead of going to the infinite trouble of compiling it here. It possesses the considerable advantage of making the reader acquainted, in a piquant manner, with many local incidents otherwise unattainable, yet indispensable, on account of their elucidating events, *when* and where these have occurred—items of importance in historical literature, and really serviceable for better comprehension of the general subject under view. Besides, as little lights of history, they are duly retained, destined of dispersing, to some extent, the gloom which is cast over the mind during the perusal of belletristic works, by their throwing an electric glare of truthfulness over the dismal pages of nightly ignorance and gory battle-fields, which latter they point out with unerring precision, and by the force of the limpid, spasmodic dazzleness peculiar to the artificial nature of that extraordinary light, awake in every one anew the hope which precedes the glorious daylight of enlightenment, that wars be altogether eschewed through an obligatory international law, and its obedience practically enforced among the nations, through the establishment of a republican form of government.

As republicanism is the highest tribunal of civilization, it wields the executive power of impartial justice to all men, mainly through the institutional or lawful provision of peace, the ethereal shield of liberty, protecting life, individually and collectively, nationally and internationally, publicly and privately, at all hazards.

In times of peace only, as obviously is the object of civilization, the individual happiness of man, to an universal extent, duly attained, in full accordance with religion, which teaches us through nature that God, creating man to live, intends him to die a natural death. To expose one's self to an unnatural death, or worse, precipitate it intentionally, is, therefore—the one a personal fault, and the other an uncivilized action—similar to insanity, hereditary or not, which, caused by disease of the vital brain, the consequence of an unwise life uncongruous of nature, proves that life stands entirely unconnected with the time of death, as so chastely and omnipotently veiled by God only. Then again, the local items above referred to mournfully serve as links in the chain of study, how far this war has detained the march of progress—although it must be admitted that any war, like sin, once committed, is a step nearer atonement, which signifies, in regard to politics, that by the ready avowal of republican institutions, as redeeming a nation from sin by freeing it from the last remnant of barbarism, may render it in future more prosperous, and each individual better and happier. In the same proportion that the Christian religion stands to Paganism, civilization to barbarism, peace to war, the quick spread of republicanism to universal popular enlightenment, so sure it is that its advance in Europe stands parallel to the influence which it receives from the United States of America. Revered by us as a political as well as private acme of justice, and accordingly practiced as a national law, in all international affairs, Peace is the Minerva of Liberty in a free country, the Aurora Australis, which lovingly animates the power of virtue, enabling man's happiness to unfold itself through life in all its pristine purity and strength, and the terrestrial temple of the soul, in which the conscience of man piously worships God. As such America introduces republicanism into the civilized world, substantiated by our greatness as a nation—the incontestible proof of man's incomparable happiness, here attained under the canopy of independence as well as of heaven.

No longer a matter of time, but of absolute certainty in this enlightened age, of succeeding in making republicanism universally appreciated, it requires but reduction of expense and of time in our steamship travel and in letter postage. The more we gain upon annihilation of geographical distances by telegraph and steam, the speedier we shall attain to the desired end of elevating all nations into political manhood, affording them proper opportunities to copy from us, as the living example. By thus constantly increasing the number of our steamers, plying between America and Europe, and the world at large, at the smaller an expense of passage and of freight moneys as practical the better, increasing likewise the speed of travel, if at all possible, as valuing time, we shall unfailingly bring about the desideratum—the great point at issue in civilization—an increase of the explanation between brother and brother, which knows of no hindrance, fears no censor—is the sunny light of reason and of love, which goes to heart, convinces, and succeeds. This reflection is drawn directly from the uncontrovertible fact that Europe has gained more in liberal ideas since the days of steamship travel, bringing it into frequent contact with America, than its progress in that direction amounted to ever since the invasion by the Huns, and which progress in the practical promulgation of civilizing principles is bound to increase in exact proportion to the tide of immigration setting in here strongly, which ebbs its fertilizing truths through the lunar agency of sublunary happiness into the hearts of all mankind, arousing them to be faithful and unfailing in their own sovereign independence as republicans.

Every information in regard to European affairs generally, received in America, whether officially or privately, it ought to be borne in mind is furnished from abroad by aliens, who as such are unfortunately biassed in the judgment of international affairs, from the very nature of their governments, as consequent upon the conventional life the people traditionally lead as rigid adherents to caste ; less indeed from ignorance and prejudice, or good intentions in many individual cases, concerning the duty of elevating man to the moral standard of social equality, than what appears to us a willful and sinful lack of determination of familiarizing themselves with, and without any more circumlocutory ado in this age, adopt our system of government, in which that standard is secured to all us a form and basis of civilization, as they have had ample opportunity afforded them during a hundred years, of doing so.

I have already shown in the introductory of this work that the German and French, as well as any other immigrant here, proves to a fault that his relatives he left behind possess to a like degree the proper fitness for self-government there, and that dire necessity no longer legitimatizes monarchical governments, where the people have by universal enlightenment emancipated themselves from an originally barbarous condition of unfitness to live peaceably and within the boundaries of law, but that, proving now to be enlightened they ought to know that government is not a compulsory institution among practically, intelligent, and unbigoted beings, but merely a clerkship of the nation, composed of every body as an integral, a natural, and an indevisable part, and should never be dreaded as an instrument of arbitrary power; on the contrary, may well and should be loved as a huge law office, in which the legitimate rights and the sacred welfare of man are in quite a fraternal manner broadly and intelligently discussed in the eyes of God.

The judgment of the powerful abroad with reference to war—resorted to in order to adjust difficulties, as if they still lived in mediœval ages, in which the rational being had not the full intellectual force of fortitude at his disposal of combating with and of controlling the infuriated senses of man and nations, constantly embarrasses us of conceiving as justly, because bloodshed never coincides with noble or brave acts, constituting enlightenment, nor ever was, or is now at this period of the world's history, in accord with civilization, in which *peace at all hazards,* in the settlement of difficulties, both privately and politically, predominates as the principal characteristic, and rises on the horizon of enlightenment as the most brilliant star, guiding man through the dark labyrinthic nights of ignorance. We therefore rigidly practice it as a nation, as in adherence to the superior wisdom, and in proper conformity of the charitable principles pervading all our institutions and industrious habits of life, confident that with the spread of republics man's unhappiness will everywhere disappear from sight altogether.

In regard to historical productions, they dwindle down to a mere clever recital of authenticated occurrences, not at all elating in themselves; on the contrary, and in reality, very pitiable in their sad consequences of so much sanguinary awfulness and general misery they entail, sternly demanding no positively necessary attention beyond tearful, and of course substantial succor, except that in every one of us it should arouse anew the one overwhelmingly sacred duty, amendatory of such misery, and incumbent upon an American to comply with, and as a man of honor and personified truth cheerfully and voluntarily to fulfill, which is to express his gratitude for our institutions, under which, in peace and amidst plenty, he, and every one, is blessed, and can live happily, who labors, acts sensibly, studying contentment and health, and which is not the case in any other nation to such an approximatingly universal extent, but should be the case the world over. Such an avowal is not only always timely, but especially so now. It strenuously draws the attention of the world upon us, in order that foreign nations be led to respect us by such a manful demonstration of a proper feeling of nationality, which, while it honors us, refutes but their stubborn unbelief in the superior merits of our institutions; it is theory practically applied. For sheer want of such morally convincing proofs they remained so deplorably long in ignorance of the manifold blessings they afford, openly derided them, even held the same in abuse for selfish purposes of their own, in no accord with either the conscience of the rulers nor the intellectual greatness of a nation so duped, showing it quite conclusively that the chances heretofore afforded them for knowing America well, and of thoroughly estimating its vast moral power, did anything but suffice.

Availing themselves of the misfortunes to man, monarchs covertly denounced republics as a conglomeration of lawlessness, when secretly at heart they fear the promulgation of the eternal truth of the equality of man's mind for culture in the eyes of the civilized world, as laying bare their position of aristocrats as untenable in this age, and pointing with decimating effect towards the ruse of the origin of their prerogatives as altogether unwarrantable, because devoid of charity and generosity to fellow-men, and as to a hereditary right to them the absurdity appearing like a dense fog, which disperses only when the sun rises—then not the shadow of a vapor remains to justify it.

A sort of tomahawk they still use in blasphemously quoting the Bible as authority of the will of God that rule and servitude should exist on earth, and cite nature as legitimatizing coercion, when from a study of the same nature we are taking quite a different version, and find that it leaves us at a loss how to conceive man irrational. Reason, therefore, by the strong, unobtrusive power of which we conceive and comprehend God's love of all mankind alike, as our bright vision beholds man living in inimitably animated forms of anatomically perfect construction and equality, leading us to the decorous demeanor of justice and kindness toward one another in the paths of private life, led us to unanimously declare our independence from man's aggression upon another's rights, and politically accomplish a gathering of free and good men, denominated the republic, which significantly includes all mankind. That its security be imperishable, and the world may readily adhere to its sacred vows, we gathered into it all the available principles which render man good, and consequently happy, so as to serve not only us for the time being, but all mankind forever.

Upon this truly religious and equally rational comprehension of God's will rests our conviction that all nations will arrive at the appreciation and adoption of the republican form of government, the time for their proclamation being fixed according to the advance reached in general intelligence by the people universally.

That in spite of the Christian religion, which the civilized world has adopted, on account of its incomparably humanizing principles, but we, and a few other but thinly populated countries, have as yet followed its divinely moral teachings, which although so near common sense, appear still so distant in time of application, proves the difficulty of the task, that without the aid of all, republican principles cannot be thoroughly appreciated, inasmuch as universal enlightenment and personal worth, based upon education, and, above all, a diffusion of a fraternal spirit of amiability and generosity are indispensable requisites for the due attainment to its desirable, ultimate end.

WM. E. F. KRAUSE.

SAN FRANCISCO, February 22d, 1871.

THE WAR.

It appears that on the 19th of July, 1870, the Emperor of the French declared war against Germany, to the great astonishment and surprise of the people of the latter country, there being no palpable reason for a necessity of any such warlike demonstration on his part. It was, therefore, quite natural that the German people united in preventing serious mischief, leaving internal controversies pending—as is always the case when a foreign foe is intermeddling or intruding. This patriotic feeling became the more intensified the more it became known, from the various pretexts advanced, proving to be shallow, that they covered nothing less than a deliberate design upon the independence and the freedom of the German people, thus forcibly reminding them of the great war of liberty in bygone days, and securing for this one that unanimous action which augurs victory from the commencement by its energetic execution, as inspired by the very holiness of the cause of "the defence of national freedom."

What these pretexts were which the Emperor of the French advanced for the inauguration of the war, and his real intentions enshrouded by them, that has to be enunciated, that the latter, although of a twofold nature, as being dynastical or personal, and political or traditional, were by him blended into one determined design of aggrandizing upon Germany.

During his entire reign the care for his throne, and a continuancy of his dynasty, has actuated his policy at home and abroad, availing himself of the influence of the church upon the peasantry, likewise of the Imperialists, and of the army, with whom the name of Napoleon bears a charm, and of the majority of the middle classes, who were his staunch supporters, because they feared anarchy. By such aids he held successfully in check the Bourbons, the Orleanists, the Liberals, and even the Republicans, always occupying the army in a manner satisfactory to their martial spirit. But ever since his transatlantic adventures in Mexico, the French nation, a liberty-loving people, began to show their sagacity by leaning towards the espousal of the republican cause, exhibiting this inborn desire to be free; in other words, independent of the rule of any man whomsoever born of woman—publicly and unmistakably—which showed Napoleon that not only had republicanism and enlightenment largely increased in France since 1848, but that his throne was tottering in consequence, and his dynasty in jeopardy of expiring. Such a calamity to his imperial self-interests he had two ways of encountering—either by war with a neighboring nation or by a plebiscitum. Both were slippery and dangerous to traverse. As to a war abroad, there was but one really popular, a war with Germany, as answering the political traditions of France. In case of victory, it would be considered by the nation as an answer received to the queries of Leipsic, Waterloo, and Koniggratz, accompanied by the Rhenish provinces, so ardently and persistently coveted, as a pledge of the sincerity of future friendship.

But be it understood, in case of victory only, that the very attempt of making victory a condition was not only hazardous in the extreme, but fatal to himself and dynasty in case of defeat; while of course by dictating peace from Berlin, his power would become indestructible from that day, as far as the arbitrary rule of a monarch can find submissive supporters in oppression. Delay, however, was out of the question, because of the imminent danger of his position, denying the difficulty and nature of available means to avert it.

The idea of going to war with Germany, so daring in itself, became preposterous when it was considered that France was not at all prepared for it. The genius of Napoleon, correctly estimating the pressure of time, therefore, abstained for the present from this mode of procedure, and adopted first the peaceable way—not, however, losing sight of the dilemma wherein he might be placed of risking at any time his fortune by war, for which untoward necessity he never flagged of preparing with consummate precision. His resolution now was taken; votes were cast, he standing well in the eyes of the world as the elect of the French people—thanks to the clergy, the prefects and the maires. Still it was not enough. A liberty-loving people require proofs, not words. Concessions they wanted, and concessions Napoleon now made. To the astonishment of France it was a new Constitution, well framed, which he gave, at the same time with a majority in the House devoted to himself which would secure for him, at all times, personal control of all important decisions generally.

In spite of these apparent successes, France was observed to be still in a ferment, the cause being that during the plebiscitum many had voted *aye* upon condition that no war should be declared; but then again—and what constituted more than his misgivings—the army, the main pillar of the Napoleonic Empire, to the figure of 43,000 strong—just about one in ten—had voted *nay*.

In the French Senate there was next observed a very obstinate and energetic minority rising to awake stormy debates, proving to Napoleon still more demonstratively the waning of his power, notwithstanding his success at the elections.

Several years had so elapsed, during which the greatest activity was displayed and persevered in to procure the necessary material for war. The preparations were upon such a gigantic scale that all the world might have guessed correctly who was meant by it, leaving nothing doubtful but the moment of time for the outbreak of war. Napoleon therefore decided upon war with Prussia and Germany, but endeavoring first to attain to the same object by diplomatic means. The object of course remained the Rhenish Provinces and the annexation of Belgium; and as the genius of Napoleon is well known to befit him more conspicuously for diplomacy than the battle-field, he tried to effect the object by diplomacy. It was as early as 1862, during the Mexican expedition, that he made the first attempt of absorbing Belgium and adjusting the Rhenish frontier with the assistance of Prussia, consulting Count Bismark anterior to the Count's acceptance of the portfolio of Prime Minister of Prussia. This defined to the world the position of France in the German-Danish war in favor of the allies. But when the Treaty of Gastein, between Austria and Prussia, was signed, he immediately changed his tactics, showing a marked unfriendliness towards the latter country, accountable for only on the fear that a too intimate friendship between Austria and Prussia would deprive him of the fruits of his diplomacy in the German-Danish war.

About the same time Bismark gave Napoleon, at St. Cloud, a general outline of his views upon Germany, while Napoleon responded with his views upon Belgium, without further comment on either part upon the feasibility of the execution of these plans. The silence of Count Bismark on this occasion, Napoleon interpreted in favor of his plans, having expected that the war between Austria and Prussia would be fought in 1865, and instantly approached Prussia with friendly overtures upon the rupture between Austria and Prussia becoming imminent—availing himself of the presence of Prince Napoleon in Berlin, as well as other confidential agents, to propose various schemes for enlarging their respective boundaries. In one case it was Luxembourgh; in another, the boundary of 1814, together with Landou and Sar-Louis; then again, touching larger objects—for instance, the territory of the French-speaking Swiss or the boundary of Piedmont to be adjusted according to the language most prevalent among the people.

All this occurred previous to the war between Austria and Prussia in 1866, and in May of that year the proposals assumed the shape of an offensive and defensive alliance, of which Count Bismark made mention in his circular of the 29th of July, 1870, the Count stating that:

Firstly—In case of a Congress, it should be unanimously declared that Venetia be ceded to Italy, and the Duchies of the Elbe to Prussia.

Second—Should these cessions not be realized, then an offensive and defensive alliance.

Third—The King of Prussia would commence hostilities within ten days from the adjournment of Congress.

Fourth—Should Congress not at all assemble, Prussia to take the field thirty days after the signatures to the agreement in question had been exchanged.

Fifth—The Emperor of the French to declare war to Austria as soon as hostilities between Austria and Prussia should have commenced; to take the field in thirty days, with 300,000 men.

Sixth—No separate peace with Austria should be made.

Seventh—Peace to be concluded upon the following conditions: Venetia to Italy; the German terrritories mentioned, footing up about seven to eight millions of population, upon choice, to Prussia; besides Federal reform in the Prussian sense of view. To France, the territory between the Moselle and the Rhine, with a population of 500,000, without the strong fortresses of Coblentz and Mayence; the section of Bavaria upon the left bank of the Rhine; the cities of Birkenfield, Homburg and Darmstadt, with a total population of 213,000.

Eighth—After the signatures to this treaty be obtained, a military convention would be agreed upon between France and Prussia.

Ninth—The King of Italy should be a party to the convention.

The number of troops with which the Emperor of the French should assist the King of Prussia, according to Article V, was mentioned at 300,000 men, and the population to be acquired by France 1,800,000, according to a somewhat superficial census.

Here, adds Count Bismark, every one more specially acquainted with the diplomacy and military history of the year 1866, may fathom the political intentions which France had in regard to Italy, with which it likewise secretly treated, and later acted upon with both Prussia and Italy. Prussia, however, firmly declining, in June, 1866, the alliance above mentioned, notwithstanding its threatening pressure on the part of France on several occasions, the French Government had now to rely upon victory of the Austrians over the Prussians and what diplomatic advantages they might secure to themselves from such a defeat. That the proposed Congress would have had the effect of allowing the three months time to elapse without affording Prussia the chance of making use of the treaty which existed betwen Prussia and Italy, is well known; likewise how France was active in regard to Custozza, to jeapardize Prussia's interests. The anything but enviable position of the French Minister of State, M. Rouher, serves as a commentary to these transactions.

From that day France never ceased to allure Prussia with projects detrimental to Germany and Belgium. The impossibility of consent of the Count of Bismark to these schemes was obvious; yet in the interest of peace, by acceding to nothing, even verbally, the Count suffered the French statesmen to enjoy their illusions delightfully, and during as much time as possible, considering that a deprivation of their hopes by way of an abrupt astonishment would endanger the peace of not only Germany but Europe, which to cherish was the decided advantage of all.

The Count was not of opinion to prevent a war with France, because it being inevitable; he counted upon Providence as unveiling the future, and was right. Even victory he considered an evil, as viewed from the high principle of civilization. He could not but calculate upon the possibility of radical changes in France and in French politics, which might altogether do away with the threatening aspect of war between Germany and France—a hope, indeed, well worthy his silence.

After the end of the correspondence with the King of the Netherlands in regard to Luxembourg, France repealed her proposals to Prussia in regard to Belgium and Southern Germany. During that conjuncture, the Benedetti manuscript was transmitted. That the French Ambassador should have committed himself, and, without authorization from his sovereign, should himself have made proposals, placing them in the Count's hands, conferring with him repeatedly, modifying the meaning of the writing, is as improbable and unlikely as on another occasion it was stated that the Emperor Napoleon never consented to the fortress of Mayence being ceded, which demand was officially made to Prussia through the French Ambassador in August, 1866, with threats of war if refused.

The various phases of French dislike and war delights which happened from 1866 to 1869, very nearly coincide with the signs of inclination and disinclination for it which the French agents thought the Count had inadvertently at times betrayed to them.

In March, 1868, at the time of the Belgian Railway trouble, Count Bismark states he was given to understand by a person of high rank, undoubtedly acquainted with former negotiations in regard to this difficulty that, in case the French should occupy Belgium—"*Nous trouverions bien notre Belgique ailleurs.*" In a similar manner, on former occasions, the Count was induced to consider that France, in a settlement of the Oriental question, could not absorb her share in the far Orient, but on the frontier.

The Count had the impression that nothing but a sure conviction that success with Prussia, to get at more territory, was impossible, would induce Napoleon to try his best to prevent Prussia having any success of the sort.

The Count had every reason to believe that, had this question not been made public, France would have *to offer* proposals to us after knowing we were ready for war, to advance upon Europe with a million of men, and carry, by force of arms, the proposals previously made, viz : to make peace either before or after the first battle, entirely at the expense of Belgium, according to Benedetti's proposals.

In regard to these proposals, the manuscript which we have possession of was the handwriting of Count Benedetti's, upon paper of the Imperial French Embassy, and recognized as such by the various Embassadors and Charge d'Affairs of Austria, Great Britain, Russia, Baden, Bavaria, Belgium, Hesse, Italy, Saxony, Turkey and Wurtenberg.

In Article I, Count Benedetti, during the first reading, passed the last sentence—putting it in parenthesis—after the Count had told him that it meant an interference of France into the internal affairs of Germany which he, the Count, could not submit to even in documents held private and in his keeping. Of his own accord he altered in Article II, on the margin, some sentence of less consequence. Lord Aug. Loftus had verbally been made aware of the existence of this document on the 24th inst, and as the noble Lord doubted it, invited him to inspect it himself. This he did on the 27th, and was convinced that it was in the handwriting of his former French colleague.

That the Imperial Cabinet to-day denies these overtures, which since 1814 it accompanied with alternating promises and threats, in order to hurry us into submission, is quite explainable as matters now stand.

This remarkable document from the manuscript of the treaty to which Signor B. refers in his dispatch, reads as follows:

H. M., the King of Prussia, and H. M., the Emperor of the French, considering it useful to strengthen still more the bonds of friendship which now happily exist between them and their respective nations as neighbors, and, on the other hand, convinced that they are dutifully obliged to satisfactorily settle questions in regard to the future of both nations, upon the result of which rests the peace of the world, have for this purpose concluded to propose the following treaty, having appointed as their respective representatives, H. M., etc.; H. M., etc.; who, after having exchanged their credentials and found them correct, have agreed upon the following articles:

ARTICLE I. H. M., the Emperor of the French, admits and acknowledges the acquisitions made by Prussia in her late war with Austria and the allies of Austria, as well as submits to the steps taken already, and to be taken, by Prussia, for the formation of a North German Union, and obligates himself at the same time to assist in maintaining it.

ARTICLE II. H. M., the King of Prussia, promises to facilitate the acquisition of Luxumbourg by France; to which end H. M. shall confer with H. M., the King of the Netherlands, in order to induce that sovereign to cede to the Emperor of the French his rights to the Dukedom for a fair compensation or in some other way, the Emperor of the French paying all costs and charges.

Article III. H. M., the Emperor of the French shall not oppose a federal union of North Germany with the States of the South, Austria excepted, which Confederacy should have a Parliament, but so formed that the sovereign rights of the divers States should be respected.

Article IV. In case circumstances should arise which shall induce H. M., the Emperor of the French, to cross with his army the frontier of Belgium, for the purpose of conquest of that country, the King of Prussia shall assist France with troops and with all his might, by land and by sea, against any other nation which should declare war to France on that account.

Article V. For the purpose of a perfect execution of the aforesaid designs, H. M., the King of Prussia, and H. M., the Emperor of the French, by this agreement form an offensive and defensive alliance between themselves, which to respect they solemnly pledge themselves; added to which their Majesties consider this alliance valid on all other occasions on which the integrity of either country might be jeopardized by a foreign foe, then to arm forthwith, being actuated by no scruples, admissible of no excuse for evading the alliance.

Annexed is given a letter of Count Benedetti to Count Bismark, with the manuscript of the treaty, as both were received from the hands of the French Ambassador.

The letter reads as follows, as published at the time in the *Staats Anzeiger*:

My Dear President: In reply to the communication which I transmitted from Nikolsburg to Paris, in consequence of our conversation on the 26th ultimo., I have received from Vichy the plan for a secret convention, of which I beg to send you the inclosed copy. I hasten to acquaint you with it, that you may digest it at your leisure. I am at your service in talking the matter over with you at any time you shall desire it. Benedetti.

Sunday, August 5, 1866.

The manuscript of the plan for this treaty reads as follows:

Article I. The French Empire again accedes to the lands which formed in 1814 the boundaries of France, and which to-day belong to Prussia.

ARTICLE II. Prussia pledges herself to obtain those lands which are on the left bank of the Rhine and belong to the King of Bavaria and the Grand Duke of Hesse, upon compensation to them for the same, and to cede possession of those lands to France.

ARTICLE III. Those dispositions which connect with the German Union such lands as are standing under the sovereignty of the King of Holland are canceled; likewise those which refer to such right to lands within the fortress of Luxembourg.

In consequence of this note an official interview took place between the Count of Bismark and the French Ambassador, in which the latter insisted upon his demands being complied with, which had been projected by him, and threatened Prussia with war if refused. Notwithstanding this, the Chancellor respectfully declined; upon which the demand upon Luxembourg was made, which likewise did not succeed; upon which, again, the more important demand upon Belgium was made, which formed the contents of Count Bismark's explanatory dispatch of July 29th, originally framed by Count Benedetti, and published in the *Times*.

All these diplomatic versions demonstrate clearly that State and personal motives were blended by France into that traditional policy which Louis XIV originated, and which ever since the great French Revolution was rigorously adhered to.

This tradition comprises points which no Government in France has ever slighted or lost sight of.

Firstly—The Rhine is the natural boundary of France.

Secondly—France is destined and therefore justified and obliged to be the leading power in Europe, and has to judge by arbitration in all political matters disturbing the peace of Europe, and considers itself duty bound to prevent other powers from doing anything without her will. This the French elaborately conceive and euphemistically and charmingly express by saying: "France marches at the head of civilization."

Thirdly and finally—As an united Germany would not only endanger, but cancel these rights, and affect the dignity and the interests of France; in other words, the two points first mentioned, it must never be allowed to unite. Every attempt at this dangerous union must instantly be stifled, destroyed, and Germany kept down at all hazards.

Shortly before hostilities commenced, the *Moniteur* expressed it exactly so: France merely intends keeping Europe in its normal condition and bring it back to its equilibrium, and is of opinion that a disunited Germany signifies an absolute division there in permanancy;

in which state of severed strength and consequent weakness of the Germans, as a nation, they, the French, have nothing to apprehend, and which opinion is even so yet to a far greater extent: they are wrong, because in preventing the consolidation of the German union, for political reasons of their own, they injure the German people, morally and materially disabling them from abolishing every remnant of feudalism, through not allowing them the necessary peace of Europe to succeed in it.

If, therefore, the German nation at large had not at this juncture found itself providentially blessed with a Bismarck, whose patriotism and unfathomable genius took hold of the matter correctly, frustrating both their designs—the motive for the prevention of the German union, as well as the motive for the war, by conferring with the present Emperor of Germany, to apply the efficient strength which his great genius knew existed in the military and their leaders, a worse misery might have been entailed upon the German people than is now lamented by the French, for reasons of the above named particularism, aggravated by the consequences of conquest, in which the uncontrollable fury of the Kabyles figures among the undefensive.

But not only to the Count Bismarck, but to the Emperor of Germany is the German nation forever indebted, who, as a sovereign, thus nobly appreciated the Count, enabling him to give full vent to and exercise his genius and allowing him to use his discretion in the above two matters—he knowing full well what such a consolidation of Germany would eventually lead to, in times of undoubted national strength and general enlightenment, beyond the present temporary absorption of the attention of the people by the war.

Returning from this digression to the balance of power in Europe, as viewed by the French nation, from their political tradition and version, it rests upon the validity and instrumentality of these aforesaid three points being maintained and adhered to. These formed, therefore, the nominal reasons advanced by Napoleon and his ministers for the legitimacy and necessity of the war about to commence.

How the Emperor of the French and his ministers managed and succeeded in making this war sufficiently popular in France so as to be sanctioned by the people and undertaken, is best seen from a protocol of Count Bismark's, which he produced during the twenty-sixth sitting of the federal council, and which was laid before the German Parliament on the 20th July. In which protocol the Count says: "The events which during the last fortnight have transpired, disturbing the peace of Europe, plunging it into war, are so well known, that but a recapitulation of facts is necessary to clearly define and comprehend the state of affairs at this moment.

"Aware of the communication which the President of the Spanish

Ministerial Council made to the Cortes on the 11th of last month, likewise of the circular dispatch of the Spanish Minister of Foreign Affairs, of the 7th inst., published in the newspapers, and of the explanation which Señor Salazar had on the 8th inst. printed in the *Mazaredo* of Madrid, explanatory of the Spanish Government having for months past negotiated with Prince Leopold of Hohenzollern for the acceptance of the crown of Spain, that these negotiations were directly made with the Prince and his father, through the medium of Señor Salazar, without participation and interference of any foreign government; and, furthermore, that it is known that finally the Prince decided upon acceptance of the proffered crown. His Majesty the King of Prussia, upon being made acquainted with this decision, concluded to let it pass, the Prince being of age could do as he liked, the more readily so as the Prince's father had given his consent to his son. Neither the Foreign Office of the North German Union nor the Government of the King of Prussia knew anything at all about it. They first heard of it through the telegram of the Paris *Havas*, of the third evening, reporting that the Spanish Government had decided upon offering the crown of Spain to Prince Leopold. On the 4th the French Charge D'Affairs presented himself at the Foreign Office. By order of his government he was pained to state that this news had been very ill received at Paris, authenticated, as it had proved to be, by Marshal Prim, and asked whether Prussia was a party to it. Upon which the Secretary of State told him that it was no affair concerning the Prussian Government, nor Prussia in a position of explaining negotiations which might have been made by or were pending between the President of the Spanish Cortes and Prince Leopold.

"On the same day the Charge D'Affairs of the North German Union at Paris had an interview with the Duke of Grammont, relative to the same subject, and in presence of Minister Olivier."

It becomes here necessary to throw into high relief the moral and praiseworthy grounds and motives, upon which stands the executive of the Spanish nation before the world, when, seeing the republic as yet impossible, the consequence of a criminal neglect of free schools, it conferred upon a Prussian Prince the alternative of the honor to accept the government over the people, the so-called crown of Spain, as the best known guarantee to the Spanish nation for the time being of a peaceable future and probably great national advantages. Therefore the French Government, in preventing the consummation of such a laudable design, by allowing political reasons and arbitrary actions to sway and impede the most noble impulses of civilization: those of an indirect and sympathetic co-operation with other nations besides their own in anxious strides towards national prosperity in general—laid bare a degree of officiousness and peevishness which will never stand the paltry excuse for self-preservation; on the contrary, does demonstrate a fund of jealousy highly complimentary to Prussia, especially after the battle of Sadowa, and still more so by the remembrance of the Prussian Government of not having remonstrated with France at the time when one of the French Princes became the son-in-law of the King of Italy and brother-in-law to the Queen of Portugal.

Fortunately for Europe, with its many warlike nations densely peopled and all votaries to past feudal glories of strife—civilization has comparatively of late astoundingly advanced in appliances and developments of arts and sciences for the purpose of destroying the opportunity that war, with all its exploits of personal bravery in self-defense, is affected to such an extent as to reduce that virtue, called personal courage to a mere reliance upon skill and strategy to butcher in bulk. The present war, of but seven months' duration, proves that a climax in the art of killing has about been reached, and by it the domineering power of France over Europe transferred to the cool prowess, practiced scholarship, and compact strength of Germany. Peace thus shielded by Germany, is now sure to the warlike millions of Europe. Germany will henceforth be to Europe what the Atlantic is to America: the safeguard against aggression. As long as monarchical surveillance shall be necessary among nations unfit to govern themselves, Germany is the country which knows how to guard peace from without and within. It will stand between and pacify Great Britain and Russia. Having taken the place of France in the balance of power in Europe, it will for many reasons always be listened to as a mediator. Therein successful, Germany is synonymous of peace — it is the guarantee for future peace to Europe. As to any other cloud arising at any future time upon the political horizon of Europe, it will give but weather lightning!

Returning to the interview which the Chargé d'Affaires of the North German Union had with the Duke of Grammont relative to the Spanish crown question, and in presence of Minister Ollivier, it is stated that the French Minister of State was on that occasion likewise chagrined at the general news. Public opinion, he averred, would pronounce against it; a transaction of so grave an importance having been held so profoundly secret by both Spain and Prussia, and now having been made public, it could not possibly be otherwise inferred but that France had been intentionally slighted. The main point at issue being indeed the most immaterial one, whether the Prussian Government were at all initiated into the affair or not, considering the magnitude of consequences as bound to issue from these proceedings. Should, therefore, the event really take place, peace would be seriously jeopardized. It therefore were highly advisable to appeal to the wisdom of the King of Prussia to withhold his approval of said combination, now that he was aware that as a secret it could serve no longer. The French Minister then considered it a happy omen that, it so happened that, Baron Werther being about to set out for Ems, could report to the king the irksome effect this affair had made in Paris, at the same time enabling Baron Werther of telegraphing at an early convenience to the French Minister any important decision arrived at in regard to and of a pacific nature to the subject. Baron Werther left Paris on the fifth. On the day of the departure of Count Benedetti—Mr. Cochery brought the Spanish question before the legislative body, but already the day after, a space of time far too brief for the reception of any return news from Ems, the Duke of Grammont responded to the interpellation of Mr. Cochery.

The Duke's answer, of course, avowed the impossibility of knowing particulars in regard to the matter, yet he declared that with due regard for Spain as a friendly neighboring nation, and respect for her sovereign right as to her conducting State affairs unmolestedly by any other nation, he, notwithstanding, could not suffer a foreign power to interfere by placing one of her princes upon the throne of Charles V. The consequences would be not only detrimental to the interests of France, but would disturb the balance of power in Europe. Upon this statement having become public, it could not be expected of the Chargé d'Affaires of the North German Union, who intended to communicate with the Duke, that he should transmit to him any dispatches at all. Instead of which he informed the German Embassy at Paris of it on the ninth, and exactly alike in substance to what the Prussian Government had on the fourth rendered in extent of information to the French Chargé d'Affaires at Berlin. It amounted to this, that the Spanish throne question did not effect the political relations between Spain and Germany, but concerned Spain alone, as far as the nature of the candidature for her throne had made it needful for the Government of that country to go outside and fill it there. Thus, in reality, it was only nominally an international affair, but practically of importance only to none but the candidate himself. It was further stated that Marshal Prim had these negotiations privately undertaken without participation by the Prussian Government, and had directly conferred with Prince Leopold, the King of Prussia not having been found willing, out of respect for the will of the Spanish nation, to influence the acceptance of the offer by a German prince.

In the meantime the French Government ordered the representative at Berlin, who happened to be on furlough at Wildbad, to repair to Ems. On the ninth the King of Prussia received Count Benedetti, although the circumstance of meeting at a watering place implied a desire on the part of the venerable King of at least not having to be too lengthily engaged in matters of State. The information which Count Benedetti then and there transmitted to the King of Prussia agreed with what the Duke of Grammont had communicated to Baron von Werther upon the same subject, amounting in substance to an appeal to the wisdom of the King not to sanction the acceptance of the Spanish crown by Prince Leopold—a decision of such moment in the opinion of the French Government that it would be enough for Europe to thereby regain its quietude. Upon which the Count was diametrically given to understand, that the disquietude existing in Europe had not been created by Prussia, nor was the Prussian Government to be blamed for it, but might at once be successfully traced into the inaccessible altitude of the legislative body of France. The troubles which the Spanish throne question had thus unnecessarily brought about, sprung from there. The volume of criticisms which had issued forth had, in its rapid course, submerged Europe, and endangered the peace of the world by its torrent of tribulations and anticipations of all sorts of hallucinations, and predictions of disastrous consequences. His (the King's) position as head of the family of Hohenzollern, was exclusively and naturally one of a domestic character, admitting of no control over the sovereign will of any of its members in regard to the actions of a prince. As to affairs of State, those stood entirely unconnected with matters of personal interest. Neither the Prince and the Prince's father had by him been interfered with, nor the honor of the acceptance of the Crown of Spain by Prince Leopold been made the basis for private speculation on the part of the royal house of Prussia.

On the twelfth instant Prince Leopold declined the candidature. The Prussian Government received the first tidings of this important step from Paris. It so happened that Baron von Werther having left Ems for Paris on the eleventh, and arriving the next day, was present at an interview which the Spanish Ambassador there had with the Duke of Grammont, upon which occasion the telegram had been produced which Prince Leopold had sent, transmitting his decision declining the honor. Upon another occasion, later in the day, the Duke of Grammont remarked to Baron von Werther that, after all, the refusal of Prince Leopold was but of accessory consequence, inasmuch as France would anyhow not have permitted the Prince to ascend the throne of Spain—at the same time laying great stress upon the slight inventively conceived to have been received at the hands of the King of Prussia, in having at all granted to the Prince the alternative of the acceptance of so important an offer without first consulting France in regard to it. However, the Duke appeared satisfied with the King of Prussia's explanation of the affair, in a letter to Napoleon, having said that in granting to Prince Leopold the alternative of the acceptance of the Crown of Spain, he had not been of opinion that the interests and dignity of France would thereby be necessarily affected. Now that the Prince had declined of his own free will, he (the King of Prussia) had, of course, acquiesced to the decision of the Prince.

The day following, at Ems, Count Benedetti, upon meeting the King, requested a confirmation of the refusal as transmitted by the Prince, and an assurance besides that, at no future time, an acceptance of this candidature by a German prince should be sanctioned by the King. From that day Count Benedetti had no more interviews with the King of Prussia.

How the Government of France could seriously view the acceptance of the Crown of Spain by a German prince as positively dangerous to France, moreover profess it as an affront to the French nation, is inconceivable, otherwise than as a pretext for finding an excuse to declare war, and for no other earthly purpose than to dim the light of a rising star. All these subtilties and evasions serve as an evidence of the culpable weakness of monarchial governments, in which the nation is debarred by law from energetically interfering and uttering at the right moment its powerful voice of disapproval, and of insisting upon a peaceable settlement through the instrumentality of law and the aid of diplomacy.

In the United States of America, such a case as was presented to the world in the shape of the preliminaries to this war, would be everywhere ridiculed. May be that boast is quite natural—the whole world could not invade America. The idea of succeeding in misling a whole nation to shoulder arms within, so to say, a day or two, betrays an ignorance on the part of all of the knowledge of common occurrences of the day, which stamps the daily press of France—the tutor of the million—as most deplorably deficient. The most plausible reason for a war against a large foe in Europe, when by somebody advanced in Great Britain, is never listened to by the nation until the Orkney Islands know as much about the legitimacy of the impossibility to avoid it as the Prime Minister himself. But England is in this respect altogether republican; it differs but in name; her monarchs are but hereditary presidents, drawing heavy salaries, though.—As it is undoubted that the King of Prussia was unofficially made acquainted with the negotiations pending between the Government of Spain and Prince Leopold; it enjoined upon him the condition of privacy when he heard of it. It being a foreign secret, officially affecting neither Prussia nor the North German Union, its non-publicity by the King to the German nation at large was decided upon as wise and proper. At the same time the King of Prussia found it equally correct in the Spanish Government that it should pursue its deliberations in search of a suitable candidate for the Spanish throne, without hesitancy and compunction as to where it should be pleased so to do, and the more independently, as the political position of Spain towards France invited this step, and in consideration, likewise, of certain personal amenities existing between Napoleon and the Southern branch of the House of Hohenzollern.

As to the interests a Napoleonic dynasty could profess to have in a Spanish national question, it confined itself to a vigilant guard against the dreaded spread of republicanism or the organization of an Orleans dynasty in a neighboring country; but to view a secret correspondence regarding the honor of the acceptance of the Spanish Crown by a German prince in the light of an intended affront by Prussia to the French nation, was, indeed, as significant of personal ambition as it was venturesome. Indeed it was too obvious that such rigor covered the existence of an ulterior design hostile to the German nation, as being not merely unwarrantable but altogether foreign to the incident. If otherwise, all the French Government had to do in order to ward off the troublesome coincidence, was to have addressed the King of Prussia in a familiarly handsome manner upon the subject, pending a satisfactory settlement in a diplomatic way, instead of which the Napoleonic Government unhesitatingly rented the peace of Europe, by the Duke of Gammont, in the legislative body of Paris, violently calling the nation to war. To declare it, and upon so frivolous a pretext as that of humbling the German nation, was, therefore, extremely impolitic and full of surmises, especially when dispassionately considered that the science of destroying human lives by tens of thousands has reached its culminating climax to perfection, in producing woe and misery to an unanswerable extent, and must end in victory of republicanism over all monarchial governments extant. A sensible proceeding, if for no other purpose truly than of making peace internationally and lawfully respected and abided in hereafter, viewing it as the first necessity of civilization.

In order to systematically arrange all the causes which have led to this memorable war, it is now necessary to produce the note which Señor Sagasta, Spanish Minister of Foreign Affairs, transmitted to the various Spanish Ambassadors abroad, announcing the decision of the Spanish Government to offer the crown of Spain to Prince Leopold. It is worded as follows:

"Your Excellency have on previous occasions been made acquainted
"with the important explanations which were transmitted to the Cor-
"tez on June the 11th, by the President of the Cabinet. In confessing
"that the steps taken to find a suitable candidate for the throne of
"Spain had been unsuccessful, he announced that he had received
"full power to continue his search to the best of his ability. He
"had at first received this authorization from the Provisional Govern-
"ment, then from the Executive Committee, and at last from the Re-
"gency.

"Fortified with such power, Marshal Prim recommenced his diffi-
"cult mission in a discreet and secret manner, anticipating success,
"and hoping to give satisfaction to the nation at large. I have now
"the gratification of communicating to you, by order of the Spanish
"Government, that at a Cabinet meeting held at La Granja, on the
"fourth, and presided over by the Regent, Prince Leopold of Hohen-
"zollern Sigmaringen has been chosen and accepted as candidate for
"the throne of Spain. Public opinion having pronounced in favor
"of this Prince, the Government of Spain is hopeful that its candi-
"date will be joyously heralded by a large majority in the Cortes as
"King of Spain. The Provisional Government which began in 1868
"shall then close.

"Yesterday, as soon as it was possible to break silence, as until now
"demanded by discretion, I telegraphed to you the decision arrived
"at by the Government, which should best meet the approval of the
"Cortes, strictly mindful of the general constitutional law of the land,
"as well as of the rules which appertain to the choice of kings. In
"requesting of you to announce this event to the Government to
"which you are accredited, I alluded to its real and political im-
"portance and significancy as unconnected with international affairs,
"notwithstanding the great influence which it necessarily must exer-
"cise upon and disclose to the Spanish nation in future.

"The extraordinary situation of the nation, as created by the Sep-
"tember revolution, had been well maintained by the Provisional
"Government until the day when the Cortes decided upon monarchy.
"From that day, however, the Provisional Government became a
"danger, because the wishes of the Spanish people as containing

"their preference had not then been realized by facts. Should,
"therefore, the Government not find means and ways of realizing this
"idea, her enemies would speedily gain ground and harass it by
"unreasonable expectations of every sort. But these difficulties have
"been obviated, thanks to the efforts made by the majority of the
"people, and by the Government—a rare occurrence, indeed, in any
"civilized nation of having been able, under similarly trying circum-
"stances, to maintain peace over two years. At last public opinion
"at home and abroad loudly demanded a radical change.

"In the interior of Spain the desire to crown the work of the revo-
"lution became great, while in foreign countries, befriended with
"Spain, the same wishes were expressed. The world required a
"guarantee for a permanent peace, as your Excellency has had fre-
"quent opportunities of ascertaining.

"This very success of which I have made mention affords the
"Spanish Government to-day an opportunity of communicating
"through your Excellency to the Government of * * *, and
"which gratifying news I doubt not will be cordially received. Both
"countries, indeed, reciprocate a feeling of sincere friendship, ani-
"mated by expectations and wishes for its permanent continuancy.
"The present Government of Spain has always exerted itself in its
"foreign relations to merit public opinion, and benefit the Spanish
"nation.

"Should Prince Leopold be chosen to ascend the throne of Spain,
"upon the vote of the Cortes, as alone invested by the people with
"sovereign power to decide upon a prince's choice, and declare him
"King, then shall he represent a constitution the most democratically
"liberal of any ever possessed of by us or by any other nation so and
"similarly governed. Although he is a foreigner, about to occupy
"the highest position in the gift of the nation, his Government will
"have less difficulty in obeying public opinion than might be inferred
"from the strange fact of he being a foreigner. From the day he
"does ascend the throne of San Fernando he shall be considered a
"Spaniard, and in a truly Spanish manner shall he continue to
"strengthen the great achievements of the September revolution.
"His energies shall be principally directed towards a complete regen-
"eracy of the nation in her internal organization in all national
"points of view, while externally he shall observe the strictest neu-
"trality in all international relationships, and shall thus be enabled
"to devote all his studious efforts to the advancement of the moral
"and material interests of the country, in order that through him the
"object may be attained of making Spain prosper. In this sense it is
"justifiable that the Government of the Regent, free to direct its
"steps according to discretion, has acted in this matter upon its own

" responsibility, and addressed Prince Leopold directly, nor reflected
" an instant upon it being honorable to avoid every influence from a
" foreign Cabinet. I beg leave to direct your Excellency's special
" attention to this point, as much depends upon it being reliably
" known that *the Government of the Regent has acted upon its own discretion*
" in furthering this plan, and so that it may be thoroughly understood
" that no national interest abroad, far less a foreign interest, has actu-
" ated the Government in pursuance of these negotiations.

" Nothing but the desire to grant the wishes of the nation, and to
" fulfill the mission which the Regent and the Cabinet Ministers had
" delineated, has prompted him to address a prince duly of age, and
" related to most of the reigning families in Europe, at the same time
" standing in no direct lineage of becoming the recipient of a special
" crown, therefore free to accept and to become the possessor of the
" one of Spain; a point of importance to the Spanish nation, that it
" might at all times feel secure against hostilities from foreign powers
" upon dynastical ground.

" Thus the candidature of the Prince of Hohenzollern Sigmaringen
" interferes in no wise with the friendly relations which Spain enjoys
" reciprocatedly abroad, nor can and should affect the interests of
" other reigning families as dynastically allied. As your Excellency
" is now assured of the intentions which animated the Government to
" decide upon this candidature, which shall be duly laid before the
" Cortes for acceptance, your Excellency will be able to act in con-
" formity with the motives which have led to these intentions and
" ultimate actions whenever an opportunity should present itself of
" explaining this event at the court to which you are accredited. I
" hold myself before hand convinced that your Excellency will zeal-
" ously convey the exact meaning of the purposes in view which have
" instigated the actions of the Government of his Highness.

" Please read this dispatch to the Minister of Foreign Affairs, and
" then hand him a written copy. May God preserve your Excellency
" many years.
    (Signed)   " PRAREDES M. SAGASTA.
" MADRID, 7th July, 1870."

Upon this document now follows the answer which the Duke of Grammont gave, July 6th, in the legislative body at Paris, upon the interpellation of Mr. Cochery:

The Duke replied that " Marshal Prim had offered the Crown of
" Spain to the Prince of Hohenzollern, and that the Prince had
" accepted the same. The Spanish people, however, had not expressed
" themselves upon that point. The French Government was not
" acquainted with the respective negotiations, and he (the Duke)

"thought best of adjourning the discussion upon this topic as alto-
"gether deficient in particulars in order to correctly judge in the
"matter. The Government would continue its neutrality, but would
"not suffer a foreign power in placing one of her princes upon the
"throne of Spain, and thus trespass upon the honor and dignity of
"France. The French Government had confidence in the wisdom of
"the German, and the friendship of the Spanish people. Should it be
"disappointed, it would know its duty without delay and weakness."

This speech was much applauded by the majority in the House, and commented upon, on the fifteenth of July, by Mr. Ollivier, viz.:

"The mode and manner in which you have received the explana-
"tions as rendered on the sixth of July, assures us positively that
"you sanction our policy, and that we could be sure of your assist-
"ance in case of emergency. We, hereupon, entered into negotia-
"tions with foreign powers, inviting them as mediators for the purpose
"of convincing Prussia of the legitimacy of our complaints. We
"have not required anything from Spain; the sensitiveness of her
"people we had no desire to evoke. We have not negotiated with
"the Prince of Hohenzollern, because we considered that Prince
"under the tutillage of the King of Prussia. We have abstained
"from commingling complaints over other matters with this particu-
"lar affair. The majority of foreign powers approve more or less of
"the justice of our complaint!

"The Prime Minister of Prussia has responded that he "knew nothing
"of this affair, nor would the Cabinet of Berlin become cognizant of
"it. We then addressed the King. The King avowing that he
"had authorized the Prince of Hohenzollern to use his own judgment
"in accepting the Crown of Spain, declared that he was not acquainted
"with the particulars of the negotiations as pending between the
"Prince of Hohenzollern and Spain, he having acted in this mat-
"ter as head of the family, and not as Sovereign. The King of
"Prussia, moreover, has mentioned that this affair had by him been
"turned over to Count Bismarck. We could not accept this answer
"as satisfactory; we could not admit such delicate distinctions be-
"tween 'head of a family' and 'head of a nation.' In the meantime
"we received from the Spanish Ambassador the news of the refusal
"of the Prince of Hohenzollern. It came unexpectedly, and from a
"direction which we had not anticipated. This happened on the
"twelfth of July, while our correspondence was going on with
"Prussia.

"We insisted that the King should second the refusal; that he
"should pledge himself not to give his sanction of the acceptance of
"the Crown of Spain by a prince of Hohenzollern, should it at any
"future time be again offered. Our demand was in itself moderate,

" and couched in an equally decorous language. We then wrote to
" Benedetti he might reiterate that we kept nothing under disguise,
" nor were searching for pretexts. The King refusing to grant this
" demand, told Count Benedetti that in this matter he preferred
" keeping his own counsel, as well as on all similar occasions, as cir-
" cumstances might arise which demanded full liberty of thought and
" action on his part.

" Notwithstanding, and out of sheer love of peace, we did not
" break off negotiation. In proportion to our forbearance, was our
" surprise great, when we heard yesterday that the King had officially
" refused an audience of Benedetti which news had come over
" from the Prussian Government. At the same time, we received in-
" formation that the Prussian Ambassador, von Werther, had been
" recalled, and that Prussia was arming. Under such circumstances
" it would have been remiss, undignified, and forgetful of duty, on
" our part, not to have made preparation for war. We have pre-
" pared ourselves to accept the challenge, leaving everybody his due
" part to enact, and responsibility to answer for; we have since yester-
" day called in the reserves and taken measures for the protection
" of the interests, the security, and the honor of France."

The conduct of Count Benedetti is best seen from the lucid description of the occurrence, and enables history to infer who really was the aggrieved party.

Count Benedetti solicited on the 9th of July, in Ems, an audience of the King of Prussia, which was immediately granted. During this interview Count Benedetti demanded that the King should command the Prince of Hohenzollern to withdraw his acceptance of the Spanish crown. The King replied that as far as this affair had developed itself, he having been applied to as head of the family, and not as King, he had not commanded the Prince to accept the candidature for the Spanish throne, nor could he now command the Prince to withdraw from the same. On the 11th following, Count Benedetti requested and was granted, a second audience, during which, he rather pressed compliance with his demands. The King replied that the Prince being of age, knew himself what course to pursue without his, the King's, interference. Besides, he knew not even the whereabouts of the Prince at present, as he had been known of late to travel among the Alps.

On the 13th, on the Esplanade at Ems, the King handed Count Benedetti an extra from the Cologne *Gazette*, just received, containing a telegram from Sigmaringen, in which the Prince, upon his own free will, refused acceptance of the Crown of Spain, and mentioned to the Count, at the same time, that not even he himself had received a communication on the subject from the Prince, although, of course, due during the day. Count Benedetti hereupon replied that he had known it already, the night previously, direct from Paris. The King now thought the matter satisfactorily settled. To his astonishment, Count Benedetti demanded of the King that he should distinctly declare himself unwilling, at any future time, to grant a similar permission. This the King flatly refused, and remained firm, although again and again importuned upon the same subject. Now Count Benedetti requested a third audience. Upon being asked by an aide-de-camp what he had of so much importance to communicate, he answered that he wished to have the honor of conversing upon the same topic as in the morning. The King refused the audience, sending him word that he had no other answer to give, and referred the Count to the Government at Berlin for further views upon the subject. Count Benedetti, wishing to leave Ems, expressed a desire to pay a last visit to the King, which was granted, the King receiving him at the railway station, before the train started for Coblenz.

From this minute description of the manner of Count Benedetti, in this affair, it might be inferred that he acted under instructions from the French Government, disguising two set purposes: the one, to either compromise the King in the eyes of all Germany and Europe, should he have acceded to their demands; or, the other, the more likely, upon refusal of their compromising demands, incense the King of Prussia to such a degree that the French Government might therefrom weave the textile fabric of a casus belli.

That there was a way of guarding dignity and right, and maintain both without having resort to war, appears to have been of unfathomable depth in the minds of French statesmen, or may be, that they considered such a possibility too unreal. Compared with them, how different the noble and dignified bearing of King William in this matter; that military, so amiable as a gentleman, not merely baffled the vileness of the snare laid for him to entrap himself in, but made it serve him in convincing the entire German nation that the intent of the insult received, was not for himself, but for the German Union. When it became known *how* he had resented that imputation, *then* the whole nation applauded him, and threw back with terrible vigor the attempt at disturbing the peace of Europe upon frivolous pretexts. From the manner in which the Duke of Grammont had answered the interpellation of Mr. Cochery, and Count Benedetti conducted his mission, there could be no further doubt as to their intention of forcing a war. The peevish manner in which the Duke of Grammont had received the news of the refusal of the Prince of Hohenzollern, corroborated it to a certainty. Another proof may be found in the following *expose* of Monsieur Ollivier:

The Duke of Grammont having declared in a conversation he had with Lord Lyons, the English Ambassador at Paris, that the refusal of the Prince Hohenzollern would smooth matters entirely in regard to the Spanish question—the London Cabinet at once endeavored to bring about a verity of the settlement. When subsequently the desired non-acceptance had been obtained, instead of expressing himself satisfied, he declared to the English Ambassador that it was very perplexing. On the one side public opinion was so aghast that he doubted very much that the Government could maintain itself beyond the morrow, if he should say the affair was satisfactorily settled, unless more satisfaction could be obtained from Prussia and produced. The very refusal of the Prince should here have ended the origin of the dispute, and settled the affair *de facto;* instead of which, the programme of war was completely rehearsed by France.

As to Spain, it could no longer be drawn into the quarrel should it come to war, as France and Prussia now only were concerned. The English Ambassador remonstrating with the Duke, the latter evasively said, that everything depended now upon the conclusion to be arrived at to-morrow, the 13th of July, at a Cabinet meeting, presided over by the Emperor, and which decision would at once be handed over to the Legislative body, and he be unable to communicate to him. It appears, however, that in the sitting referred to, no resolutions were arrived at, for the Duke of Grammont had to announce to the Legislative body: " that the negotiations which we continue with Prussia, " and which at no time embraced another point, have not, as yet, " been concluded."

To the Ambassador of the North German Union, Baron von Werther, the Duke of Grammont unburdened himself, on the 12th of July, without restraint. The refusal of the Prince of Hohenzollern he considered, as before stated, of very little importance, inasmuch as the French Government would have anyhow prevented his ascension to the throne of Spain; it was the secret manner in which it had been done, which had vexed him, and he feared would create an ill feeling between the two nations. Moreover, he actually demanded a letter from the King apologizing to the Emperor; proposed contents; in short, became so ludicrous, and at the same time autocratic, as to make one think that he had suddenly transplanted himself into the days of Louis XIV. The *exposé* of Minister Ollivier on the 15th of July, the day on which the French declared war against Germany, was no less peremptory. Introducing the subject, he said: " We " have not required anything of Spain, nor are willing to touch the sen- " sibilities of the Spanish nation. Then in regard to the permission " given by King William to the Prince to use his own judgment in ac- " cepting the crown, and to the demand made by France to withdraw " that permission, he said: " We could not receive the answer as "satisfactory, it being too subtle a distinction for us to acquiesce "to father of the family and father of the nation," which plainly proves, inasmuch as the distinction between one and the other is not at all subtle, or could not be readily acquiesced to, that *Napoleon* wanted war at all hazards.

Throwing all the blame for the war upon Prussia, because the King had not received Benedetti, that "the Prussian Ambassador had been "recalled, and Prussia was arming," Ollivier wound up by saying: "We are prepared to accept the war which is offered to us." Upon which the Germans answered the French as did the Romans the Carthagenians: "You will have war—well, war you shall have!"

PART THE SECOND.

NAPOLEON'S CALCULATIONS,

AND THE

DECLARATION OF WAR.

When Napoleon had decided upon war against Prussia and its probable allies, four years had elapsed during which time he had prepared for it. He had minutely weighed his resources and those of his antagonists, considered and reconsidered the alliances which might possibly be his; in short, thought of having omitted nothing which might debar him of success.

In the first instance he counted upon the enthusiastic and excitable nature of the French people. He thought the very chance offered to regain the so-called "natural" boundary of France should add new glory and new honors to the "great nation" of Europe, wipe out the blots of Leipzig, Waterloo and Sadowa, and secure still more lastingly the ambition of France to be the guardian of Europe; all these points he thought would silence the various factions in the country, inimical to, and endangering his dynasty, and would bring back to him the army in admiration and devotion, without which, he well knew he could not guard his throne against the republicans.

In this he was mistaken. The France of 1870 was not the France in the sense of the first Napoleonic empire, the less so as he had not the power the first Napoleon wielded, which, however, was necessary to convince all parties of the intelligence of his grand idea, and of the justice of the cause, for which the war should be fought and lives and property risked and staked. Instead of which, factions increased, stormy debates in the Legislative body became frequent, the demand arose for him to abdicate, without desire, "in favor of his son," as the latter was not even mentioned. Of course this demand originated with the Republicans, but the Orleanists were equally demonstrative, although silent upon their aim. This in their stead did the Empress Eugenie, who openly said that Napoleon's fall would install the Orleans. From the ranks of the army it was occasionally predicted that even the outbreak of war would not better Napoleon's position. A French officer, later in captivity, said to a German: "Oh, you and your army know well what you fight for; you go to war to carry out a fixed idea; but we fight to gratify the whims and caprices of two ladies. He meant the Empress Eugenie and the Ex-Queen Isabella of Spain."

The second consideration of Napoleon comprised the dissensions which jealousy created among the many German sovereigns and various political factions. He had assiduously exerted himself to find out the exact truth in regard to it, which has become well known through the French Embassy at Stuttgart in Wurtemberg, which propounded 41 questions on the subject, as follows, which proves his Napoleonic designs:

1. How were the parties situated in Wurtemberg previously to the war of 1866?

2. What changes have the events of 1866 produced in these parties.

3. How strong is the Democratic party; how strong the Catholic; how strong the Prussian or Union; how strong the Anti-Prussian or Conservative party?

4. Which is their *modus operandi* of gaining strength? Who are the leaders among these parties, who are the most influential persons? What newspapers have they got?

5. Which party has gained the most popularity and has the best auspices for future success?

6. What are the views of the various classes of society?

7. Is the dynasty popular? Has it a party of its own? Would these risk everything to defend it?

8. Are there any political events of note which have transpired since 1866?

9. What are their principle laws, duly passed by both Houses?

10. How do the parties in the first House confront each other since the war? How in the second House?

11. What effect has the new army organization had upon the people? What the duty on tobacco? on salt? and what views in regard to the loan?

12. How do the people like the new law of election? and how do they regard universal suffrage?

13. What will be the effect of it in future?

14. What is the opinion of the people in regard to the organization of the army? and in how far has it been successful?

15. What is the situation of Wurtemberg in point of advance in industry and commerce?

16. What effect have the late events had upon commerce and industry?

17. Has general prosperity increased?

18. What is the amount of the annual value of their exports at present? and of their imports?

19. What effect have the events of 1866 had on 'Change?

20. The most important event of the last two years is the tariff discussion. What do the people think and say of it? Do they predict for it a future?

21. What is the cause of the defeat of the Prussian party during the tariff elections?

22. Why did they not succeed in a Southern German Union?

23. What creates the jealousy among the Southern German States? (divise?)

24. Are the material interests of the South such as to be hazarded by a formation of a Southern Union?

25. Are the general interests of the South identically those of the North? Can these at all be separated? What are these interests?

26. Are there not affiliations of reciprocated interests between South Germany and Austria.

27. Could it not be made at all possible to create a vast commerce between the East and the West: between South Germany and the countries bordering on the Adriatic?

28. What is the Prussian policy in regard to the Southern German States?

29. Has it abandoned the idea of the Union of Germany?

30. Why does Austria not try to regain its influence in South Germany?

31. What policy does the present Government in Wurtemberg pursue? What is its position towards the other parties? Towards Prussia? towards Austria?

32. Does it regret the alliance, offensive and defensive, with Prussia?

33. In case of war would Wurtemberg be an ally of Prussia?

34. In case of war with Prussia would France find allies in the South of Germany?

35. Is the devotion of the Wurtemberg army great?

36. Why does the Wurtemberg Government persist in prussianizing (prussianiser) her army still more?

37. Does the Government seek entrance into the North German Union?

38. What are the political views and general tendencies of the principle members of the Cabinet?

39. What political influence does Queen Olga enjoy?

40. Does Russia befriend and assist Wurtemberg?

41. As matters now stand, can this state of affairs last? Does it lead to some non-chimerical predictions in future?

Upon these forty-one and other similar queries, the respective French *charge d'affaires*, must have answered, more or less, suitable to the plans of the Parisian Cabinet. With how great a certainty the French Government counted upon the alliance of the South German States with France, in case of war with Prussia, and upon what motives it thought the various South German Governments would be thereto prompted, may be partially seen from the ebullition of temper which Count Moosburg, French *charge d'affaires* at Carlsruhe, Baden, gave vent to, in a fit of diplomatic indiscretion, when, hearing of a declaration of war by Bavaria to France, he finally ejaculated: "I cannot understand it :—The Emperor Napoleon meant it well with the King of Bavaria, and intended to assist him in enlarging the boundaries of his Kingdom." This episode shows, more than anything, the want of penetration on the part of the French agents in correctly fathoming public opinion, and the advanced and enlightened patriotism of Germany, as it had of late matured: mainly owing to free and good public schools, and the influence everywhere in Europe, and especially in Germany, from the United States of America, as the model of nations, in which, above all other proofs of civilization, the National Union is sacredly revered and defended by the people as an imperishable bulwark of solid and invulnerable strength.

Entirely owing to incorrect views upon progress in Germany, the French Cabinet was lulled into the belief that the same animosity existed among the German Princes, which facilitated the military achievments of the First Napoleon there, and, consequently now would those of Napoleon III. The Parisians, far too exclusive citizens, seldom going outside of beautiful France, nor the reminiscences of her past glory, thought little of Germany from 1813 up to 1848; somewhat more since 1864 and 1866, until now, when enlightenment upon the general progress of the world forces itself upon them in rather an eclatant manner. Another misguidance was, that the French Government thought the newly acquired provinces of Prussia maintained still a traditionally barbarous idolatry of discontent and envy among themselves. The belief originated from Hietzing, where it was taken for granted that the Hannoverians, the Nassau people, the Hessians, the people of Schleswig-Holstein, and the citizens of Frankfort-on-the-Main would hail with delight the victorious French armies, and would be found anxious to free themselves from the nick-named "Prussian Yoke." This additionally tended to encourage the French Government in expecting success without adequate efforts; in short, to see the days of the first Empire repeated, culminating in the dictating of peace at and from Konigsberg, and similar hallucinations. Then again, Napoleon III relied upon Denmark and Austria as his allies the moment war should be declared. He considered both as naturally allied to his cause, as they were hereditary enemies of Prussia, falling short, however, in his reckoning by not reflecting upon the situation in which both Denmark and Austria were placed. He anticipated some diversion on their part, advantageous to French arms, but never anticipated they would not fight. Denmark, he thought, might have ventured it by risking the fortunes of war, although, alone, it was too weak, and the aid which France could so give, confined to naval attacks only. Neither had Sweden an interest in so doing; by becoming an ally of Denmark in a war with Prussia setting aside the probability that in rotation Russia would have attacked Sweden.

Both Sweden, as well as Denmark, were therefore forced to remain neutral, unless the latter had been indiscreet enough in taking a course by which it would have risked its very existence.

Of Austria it was supposed an alliance with France might be expected; but the internal condition of that country, at that time, kept a strain upon its ability to do so. Besides the Austrian German provinces always stand by Germany. As to Hungary, it did not even listen to an alliance, as Russia might have found a pretext for unceremoniously absorbing Galicia. Nor had Austria recovered from the shock of 1866 ; her army was not prepared to front an antagonist, well armed and but lately victorious ; her treasury was likewise not sufficiently encouraging to undertake a war against Prussia ; and as to internal dissensions respecting her crown lands, those were constant and alarming: in fact have gained an importance that the prosperity of Austria is, through them, seriously retarded, and its freedom of action paralized.

From these remarks it may be seen that Louis Napoleon was disappointed as to those aforesaid alliances. No less was he in error in regard to the two great powers of Europe—Great Britain and Russia. England, he thought, might become his ally on account of Hanover ; yet it was not so: England does not go to war frivolously with civilized nations. And as to Russia, the Emperor of all the Russias answered the French Embassador, upon being asked permission to transmit the Czar's well wishes for the French arms, " My wishes for France go by way of Germany." As to Italy, it remained neutral because the people were found unanimously in favor of Germany, while the Government was in favor of France, a very dangerous devise, indeed, to be abruptly disrespected. Even Turkey remained neutral.

Great Britain and Russia, the two leading European powers, besides a united Germany and France, were found disinclined to declare themselves enemies of Germany.

Great Britain in thus regretting the still existing yet tiresome alliance with France, which had led to the treaty of Paris of the thirtieth of March, 1856—nothing shorter than an epitaph upon the graves of the Scottish Greys at Balaklawa, and others then and there uselessly slain—truly the bitter cup of a political blunder of not having allied herself at the time with modest but substantial Prussia, kindred to her in race and religion, instead of heterogenious, vain-glorious France, unnatural to her feelings and traditions—the sure precursor of the natural consequence of such a mistake as "the thirteenth of March, 1871," plainly denominated the "Pontus boundary question ratified." By whom? Russia and Turkey, and Germany, France, Austria, and Italy. And where? In London! as it should have been done already, in 1855, peaceably, instead of upon the Malakoff.

This great power remained passive during this terrible war of 1870. She had no further desire to uphold a dynasty which she once was most vigorously active in destroying, and regarded as forever banished far into the broad bosom of the Atlantic, until suddenly and completely beguiled by Gallia. England's Pitt, Fox, Canning, or the later Palmerston, unfortunately no more, proud Albion was weak, and yielded to the syren. But the English nation soon rued its unheard of sentimentality when it saw arise, right opposite Portsmouth, another's—a *friend's*—formidable Cherbourg, from which Napoleon intended, after the programme of having conquered Germany, to invade England. So she thought correctly—better late than never—and stood aloof. Moreover, the shadow of old Blucher, and others of Waterloo and Blenheim memory, during the period of this war, having suddenly reappeared at Sadowa in the person of the greatest strategist of this century, named "General Moltke," and better informed by her own child than France was through Colonel Stoffel, of the true and solid growth and strength of Germany in enlightenment and moral courage, she felt the proper sympathy for Germany, thought of sweet home of old England, was wise and remained there, quietly watching her daughter and a little fosterling across the Channel, to Ostend. In spite of Earl Granville's ignoble remark, on the nineteenth of July, that the French would visit Berlin in three weeks, the once staunch allies of Prussia at Waterloo, the British nation, repudiated the idea, and respectfully begged leave to be excused from believing any such or similar nonsense. The British know why Prussia has to be a military nation—why its stern discipline. The interpellation of D'Israeli's premising a secret understanding between Russia and Prussia, as having existed anterior to the war, was decidedly spiritualistic, and too infidel altogether, for a sagacious and powerful nation like the English to be intimidated by. Besides, Great Britain had internally changed very much, indeed, since her unnatural alliance with France, which has served Napoleon in his phantastic designs at the expense of British lives in the Crimean war, and England nothing whatever, because, neither Suez nor even Constantinople are the keys to India, but Aden and Massowah only, which it is not likely that all Europe will touch. As to entering India *via* Persia, although feasible at various points, Persia first would have to be conquered by Russia—too remote a day to now expect its consummation—setting aside the ease with which Great Britain could at all times land her armies on Persian soil *via* Herat in the North, as well as *via* the Straits of Ormus in the South.

Routes like the Paropomisan Mountains, leading into the extreme north of Afghanistan, through interminable deserts first, ere these are reached on such an Hannibal adventure, are too impracticable to be even thought of without railroads of infinite extent traversing the dreary steppes of independent Turkey, and innumerable steamships to be built on the Volga, and crossing the Caspian Sea towards the South, before even the inhospitable mountains itselves shall come in sight of by the Russians.

The powerful influence of England in Europe, as formerly wielded by an ambitious aristocracy, requiring heavy sacrifices, but somewhat recompensing the nation with their successes, is felt no longer. The first Parliamentary reform bill forced the aristocracy to a division of power with the gentry, upon which ensued the second Parliamentary reform bill, which even now is but a few years old, and suits the people so well, that, should Gladstone's bill pass concerning secret elections, and waving of costs at elections, there can be no farther doubt of the national party coming into power. With such a change it is no wonder that her international policy is materially altered, general interests of humanity predominating with Manchester men, eschewing traditional military glory. Instead of war—diplomacy, free schools, *versus* general uncharitableness. None of the people censured the parties who sold arms and ammunition to the French, although it increased the misery and prolonged the agony of the inglorious ally of the Government, but solvent customers withal. Wise people all over the world are in the habit of making a little something by the folly of others; in fact, are necessitated in the very face of civilization to counteract a stagnated commerce and the robbing of a virtuous peace by accelerating the end of war. It is one way, a new and very radical one, this methodical killing by the ten thousand, which is bound to put a stop to quarreling, outrooting wars altogether. It will serve as a preventive, horrid as it is, until the blessed school book shall have enlightened the million to feel its abhorrence, and so keenly as to shun it as a barbarous way of settling difficulties, having made man to man sufferable in daily social intercourse, amiable and law-abiding.

In the hands of Germany, at least, the weapon of war is safe. A hard task, though, to keep peace among two hundred and eighty millions upon so small a ground as Europe, unless assisted in by the working people, who form the millions and are the soldiers to be killed, that they connect to denounce every war except leading to republican independence.

Upon the pages of history the Anglo-French alliance is but a waste of sixteen years; to Great Britain, however, an everlasting lesson that the power of civilization is vested in the Germanic race mainly, to which she and her colonies America, and Germany belong. Their triumvirate directs the intellectual and physical world, shields Christianity against barbarism, worships God from the innermost soul, and gives readiest access of free schools to the poorest of the poor, encircling and comprising all.

Like the American Union succeeded in quieting the Rebellion, even the French Republic has since execrated hers, so has Germany at last succeeded in baffling the equivocal designs of past monarchical France in regard to Southern Germany, and neither Great Britain nor Russia shall ever regret their neutrality, which enabled the Southern German States to appreciate Prussia, and her disinterested national policy.

As to Russia, the immediate and formidable neighbor of Germany, it was natural that Prussia should have been anxious to secure her neutrality by expressing a willingness to assist in pushing aside the Pontus treaty, so humiliating to not only the Czar, but the entire Russian nation. But of a further understanding than this, between the two nations' history has no clue. Russia's policy in regard to Germany has been quite logical. Her boundaries on the Baltic are not sufficiently wide, although she succeeded during the last century in conquering from Sweden several provinces, which annihilated the supremacy of the Swedes upon the Baltic; yet she was not sure of Germany uniting with Denmark for the purpose of blockading the Baltic so as to hinder her free egress. As long as Germany was disunited, it of course was impossible; the several single German States, even when united with Denmark, would not have been able to cope with Russia. On the other side, Denmark could not possibly have pursued an anti-Russian policy and united with one or the other of the German States as long as in possession of Schleswig and Holstein, which necessitated her intention to embrace an anti-German policy, in which she relied upon Russia to assist her in securing possession.

Russia, like France, uncharitably trusting in the disunion of Germany, thought Schleswig and Holstein, an integral part of Denmark, the German provinces of Russia, Russian; Hanover, English; The

Dutch, a distinct nation, Holland; the Flemish people, Belgium; and Alsace and Lorraine, French; 14 millions Germans of the Austrian empire of 34 millions population, Austrian—leaving out Switzerland, which stands aloof—a republic. But Russia, when recovered from the shock of 1812-15, had been perfectly absorbed until 1856 by the attention she had to bestow upon the consequence of the war of liberty of the Greeks, and felt herself too weak to declare war against the German Union without an ally, with the problematical issue in view of becoming mistress of the Baltic. Therefore she abided by the dictation of the Congress at Vienna, which enabled her to serve as umbrage to both Prussia and Austria. The war of 1863-64 against Denmark by both Prussia and Austria, threw Russia, in common with France, off the track. No nation comprehended the policy of Prussia endeavoring to accomplish the German Union without Austria. In the Austrian-Prussian war she hoped France would join Austria, so that Russia joining Prussia, might after the war, together with France, as being equally anxious to prevent the consummation of the German Union, frame conditions detrimental to the cause of Germany. But France was engaged with Italy, and absorbed in the reorganization of her own army, so that Russia was obliged, together with all other nations, to observe the issue of the war without solicited interference. The interests of both nations, Russia and France, collide the least of any in Europe. The war in the Crimea changed somewhat this *enteinte*. Russia's war, in Palestine, with France, assumed dimensions which did not suit France. Although careless as to Russia's progress in Turkey, if satisfactorily recompensed, after peace was declared at Paris-France was prevented by Great Britain, the avowed antagonist of Russia, to ally herself more closely with Russia. The battle of Sadowa, alarming both Russia and France, these nations tried hard to seduce the Southern German States to infidelity and unfaithfulness towards the Fatherland of the Germans, and to strengthen Austria in her ancient German policy. Suddenly France declared war in 1870 against Prussia. Impatient, and not properly prepared, though sufficiently informed by Colonel Stoffel of the military strength of the North German Union, it became evident that the rash act itself emanated from Paris alone. The dynasty of Napoleon waning, the nation nevertheless became clamorous for outside transactions. How Napoleon and the French nation were both doomed to disappointment, history has shown. Russia not prepared and in want of all communicative aid, remained neutral; an alliance with France was by no means sure to lead to victory over Germany, so that she should become sole mistress of the Baltic and gain France over to her plans in the southeast of Europe. As one of the great powers of Europe, Russia, like Great Britain, was fully aware that the victor in a German-French war would change the balance of power in Europe. Yet, in a European war at large, her interests seriously collided with those of Great Britain, and knowing that Germany was anxious to fight it out alone with France, while France tried hard to give the war the dimensions of a European one, she, like Great Britain, remained neutral at the risk which she could not obviate, of losing some of her political prestige among the nations of the world.

The fact of the neutrality of Russia, as well as that of all other large nations, explains the sympathy for Germany all over the world. Victor over France without any aid whatsoever, it blots out the pages of the history of the First Napoleon, which the French themselves have thrown into eternal oblivion by the destruction of the Arc of Triumph, demonstrating thereby that France has sworn fidelity to the Republic, and by that simple act elevated herself to a higher standard of civilization than any other nation in Europe, with the exception of Switzerland, has as yet *de facto* reached and enjoyed.

The neutrality of Austria, since the battles of Sadowa and Königsgrätz was added to the neutrality of Russia: The one of Italy by the desire for Union, and universal education, by means of free schools throughout all other Catholic countries, upon the American and Prussian plan. As in nations, so in individuals throughout the world: the intelligent and well informed have sided with Germany, to the credit of civilization and their own honorable impartiality; and be it well understood, that not only the various Governments, but the great million were imbued with the necessity of Germany superseding the power of France so as to hereafter afford peace as the principal condiment of civilization, for the purpose of paving the way to European Republicanism. No better proof is more convincing or can be more gratifying than that the vast millions of Germany at least possessed this understanding of their real interest in this war as well as knew of the more cosmopolitan advantages which would accrue to them from victory, than was demonstrated by the mechanics and working classes of Gratz, Austria. At a time much later in the history of the war, when victories had been obtained (thanks to the love of right and justice of the Germans) their courage and enlightenment in mastering beforehand their own ancient and now forgotten feuds and passions—those Austrian mechanics issued a manifest to United Germany which augurs extremely well for the peaceful future of their common fatherland. A nation composed of such bone and sinew may now already vie with America, for there is no longer any chance for either extreme : rebellion or despotism, dismemberment or treachery. They said, " In consideration that it has become " apparent that the developments of liberty and the rights of nations

"can be secured only through a permanent European peace, of
"which a powerful and invincible Germany is the guarantee now and
"forever, and in consideration that the French nation has availed
"itself of its former supremacy of power, to enfeeble all other nations,
"blaspheming liberty while the Germans have totally excelled them
"by cosmopolitan views of life, and the exercise of justice in political
"matters,

"*Be it Resolved*, by the German Republican (democratischer Club*)
"that the welfare of mankind, the developement and security of lib-
"erty, require that Germany brings the present war then only to a

---

* The democracy of Europe comprises the republican element there, after the American definition of radicalism in party sentiment here, but, in monarchies abroad, is, of course, not lawfully enacted, therefore, without revolution, remains secret and ineffective in public.

The confusion of these names, Democracy and Republicanism, does great harm in America, where the brave immigrant landing upon our blessed shores is beguiled by the name only of voting, in due time of citizenship, the democratic ticket, not knowing that ticket is legitimately subdivided, and does not alone and exclusively embody the principles of American or lawful republicanism, nor that freedom necessarily signifies an unanimous sentiment in regard to the manner and means by which liberty in a free country reaches, is enacted and enjoyed of by everybody. Not being aware of either that there should be a republican party necessary besides a democratic one, for the better working of the machinery of government, he, upon hearing of it, often remains prejudiced, through the force of habit, against the republican party, imagining that, after all, the latter may signify a tendency, like in bondaged Europe, towards lawlessness and rebellion.

That both the democratic party as well as the republican, with their many minor subdivisions, more or less radical, constitute harmonious and integral parts of the sworn and legitimate Republic of the United States of America at large, *versus* and in eternal distinction and defense of, against monarchism and blood aristocracy of the world, synonymous, the latter with hereditary and concrete imposition upon justice, through criminal neglect of duty to alike educate the people ; as well as through the upholding of exclusive privileges of man to the palpable detriment of the rights of fellow-men, from a religious and charitably humane and equitable point of view, he, the emigrant, does not at once entirely comprehend, nor that democracy differs from republicanism in minute form and various axioms of conservatism.

Inexperienced why it is absolutely necessary that both parties should here exist, in order to separately, at the polls, yet conjointly in force, fully draw out the strength of the mind and will of a free and independent citizen and voter, who constitutes the American nation at large, it may be useful to foreigners to here state that thereby the Government is effectually prevented from at any time relapsing into a barbarous incongruity and European idolatry, insidiously undermining the strength of justice and of right, so put in imperishable republican form, and now nearly centennially ancient.

Inasmuch as truth is in itself imperishable as characterizing the inimitable works of Creation, in our species is founded in and is perpetuated by a well-drawn-out and hourly more cultivated reason, so is mankind redeemable to republicanism through civilization, in no matter how many ages to come. The principle is the only correct one because it is the principle of Life—heavenly ordained, blissful, and eternal.

" close, concludes peace then only when by it the unrepublican war-
" like power of France is forever broken, as of no use whatever to
" civilization. Germany receives back Alsace and Lorraine, and a
" state of affairs is created which shall entrust Germany alone with
" the leadership over the great family of European nations, and the
" guardianship over European civilization."

As the aforesaid are the sentiments of laboring men in German Austria, sentiments thoroughly honest, it becomes a matter of certainty that fourteen millions Germans shall ere long be added to the great collective Union of Germany, nor would it be just and equitable not to recover the German Russians and old Germanic Holland, which Germany reveres of old, and which is essentially necessary to a united race and fatherland. If the King of Prussia can lay down his crown upon the German fatherland, the King of Holland can, and others, as the Kings of Bavaria, of Saxony, of Hanover and of Wurtemberg have done. In regard to England, the greater the power of Germany the greater the friendship of Great Britain, as identical with progress, and her best security for India in future; besides Queen Victoria's daughter will be Empress of Germany as long as Emperors are at all necessary for guiding an enlightened nation, which is rapidly advancing in fitness to guide and govern itself. France—a republic, England is no longer forced to add her strength to the maintenance of peace in Europe. She is now ready to follow America in the enjoyment of the colossal material advantages accruing to her vast domain all over the world from the blessings of permanent peace. Europe begins fully to comprehend the principle of the republican form of government, as exemplified in the United States of America, a cosmopolitan nation, where peace is lawfully abided in under all international circumstances occurring; although, with two hundred and eighty millions Europeans, instead of forty millions in the United States, and numerous war-like aggressive neighboring nations to contend with, and at a few day's notice, instead of none at all, and isolated withal, it may yet take ages in Europe to achieve what the United States have already enjoyed with perfect impunity nearly a century. And as to Europe so soon disarming previously to a far more universal state of enlightenment in the million, than exists after all this day, such a blessing to the people's prosperity can unfortunately, as yet, but be implored.

The most annoying of all circumstances to Napoleon, had been that he was necessitated to withdraw his troops from Rome, because in a war with Germany he could not spare their number.

By this step he offended the priests, without whom, he could not do much, and whom he expected should at this particularly critical moment be his most valuable allies.

When these reflections are recapitulated, none of which arguing success, and Napoleon is, nevertheless, known to have declared war, it becomes evident that he relied, for reasons of his own whether or not, upon victory, and that he fancied the French army superior to the Prussian in the same proportion as the Prussian army had proven itself superior to the Austrian. Again, it is owing to his incompetent military agents in Germany, who have thus served him scandalously. Colonel Stoffel explained to him from Berlin, that the Prussian innovations upon military organizations were disadvantageous, therefore advantageous to France. Thus, Napoleon anticipated the whole war to become a delightful military promenade to Berlin and beyond, halting at Konigsberg, where peace would be declared. Connected with these illusions rose the hope that, after the first victory should have been obtained the South German States would desert Prussia, the newly annexed provinces of Prussia would rebel and revolt, and Denmark and Austria, encouraged by the success of the French arms, appear on the scene of action as aiding participants.

Buoying himself up with this hope, Napoleon now framed his famous declaration of war to Prussia, which arrived in Berlin on the 19th of July, and reads as follows:

" The undersigned *Charge d'Affaires* of France, in execution of the
" command received from his Government, has the honor of commu-
" nicating to His Excellency the Minister of Foreign Affairs of His
" Majesty, the King of Prussia, that the Government of His Majesty,
" the Emperor of the French, in viewing the plan of placing a
" Prussian Prince upon the throne of Spain as hazardous to the ter-
" ritorial security of France, has been necessitated to demand of His
" Majesty, the King of Prussia, the assurance that such a combination
" should not be realized with his consent. As His Majesty, the King
" of Prussia has refused to extend this assurance, and moreover, has
" given the *Charge d'Affaires* of His Majesty, the Emperor of the French,
" to understand that, he would act in this case, as well as in any
" other similar emergency, according to circumstances possibly arising
" and influencing his decision, the Imperial Government of France
" cannot but suspect from the declaration of the King of Prussia that it
" covers a design hostile to France as well as jeopardizing the balance
" of power in Europe. The aforesaid declaration has even been
" aggravated by the announcement to the various Cabinets of the
" refusal to receive the *Charge d'Affaires* of the Emperor and to
" further animadvert upon the question.

" In consequence of which, the French Government considers it a
" duty, broaching no delay in its execution of defending its honor
" and of guarding its injured interests, and is determined for this
" purpose to avail itself of all strenuous measures demanded by the

" situation. It therefore declares itself from this day at war with
" Prussia.

" The undersigned has the honor of assuring His Excellency of
" his highest esteem and regard."

   (Signed)   LE SOURD.
BERLIN, July 19, 1870.

Before commenting upon the declaration of war and the consequence arising therefrom, it becomes necessary to refer to that episode when first the *Times* brought to light Napoleon's policy, to which Count Bismarck responded, and then what interesting developments the case divulged. A synopsis of the French and German army organization is likewise necessary in order to portray correctly and vividly the events which followed.

The moral defeat which the Parisian Cabinet had sustained by the publication of the projected treaty with Prussia had been too great, and the impression it had made upon neutral powers too extraordinary as that France should not have made every imaginable effort of placing the matter in a different light. In order to bring this about the following letter of Count Benedetti to the Minister of Foreign Affairs was published in the *Journal Official:*

                 " PARIS, July 29th, 1870.

" DUKE:—No matter how unjust may have been the criticisms to
" which I saw myself exposed, when it became known in France
" that the Prince of Hohenzollern had accepted the Spanish Crown,
" I have not deemed it fit and proper to confront them. My duty
" commanded me to leave the trouble to the Imperial Government of
" setting those criticisms right. I cannot, however, indulge in that
" same silence considering the use which Count Bismarck has made,
" of a document to which he endeavors to attach an importance
" which it never had, and I entreat Your Excellency to explain every
" solitary fact with minute precision. It is well known everywhere
" that Count Bismarck before and during the last Prussian war with
" Austria, had been found willing of assisting France in annexing
" Belgium, if France returned the civility to Prussia by allowing her a
" similar compensation in the direction of territories coveted by
" Prussia, which since then have been acquired. The whole European
" diplomatic body could bear witness, as every member became cog-
" nizant of it. The Imperial Government has constantly refused
" these offers, and one of its predecessors, Monsieur Drouyn de
" l'Huys, is in a position to explain it, and in a manner that can leave
" no doubt. When peace had been concluded at Prague, and con-
" sidering the excitement which prevailed in France consequent upon
" the annexation of Hanover, Kurhessen, and the city of Frankfort-

"on-the-Main, by Prussia, Count Bismarck again expressed his great
"desire of amending the balance of power thus gently shaken by his
"acquisitions. Different combinations they were, to be sure, not
"concerning lands bordering upon the frontiers of either France or
"Germany, which had become the topic of several interviews, in all
"of which Count Bismarck endeavored to obtain preference for his
"personal ideas. To one of these interviews I consented, in order to
"be better able to comprehend his combinations thoroughly, and
"copied, so to say, what he dictated. The form as well as the con-
"tents of that manuscript proves plainly that it has been my purpose
"to confine myself to sketching the project as it had been conceived
"and developed itself. Count von Bismarck retained it, wishing to
"transmit it to the King. I, on my part, immediately communicated
"the contents, precisely and correctly as they were given to me, to
"the Imperial Government.

"The Emperor refused these schemes immediately. I must say
"that even the King of Prussia did not approve of their basis, so that
"ever since, viz., during the last four years, I have not compared notes
"and exchanged ideas with Bismarck upon the topic above mentioned.
"Had the initiative to any such agreement been taken by the Im-
"perial Government, the copy of the manuscript would have been
"retained by the Ministry, so that I would have been unable to pro-
"duce a copy written by myself. Besides which, it would have been
"revised, and would have afforded an opportunity of entering into
"negotiations upon the subject, which would have been carried on
"simultaneously in Paris and in Berlin. In such an event, you may
"rely upon it, Count Bismarck would not have been satisfied with
"publishing its contents in an indirect way, especially at a moment
"when your Excellency set to rights other errors, which were inten-
"tionally circulated—by inserting the dispatches in the *Journal Offi-
"cial*. But to attain to his end, viz., to mislead public opinion, and
"to be ahead of any little indiscretion which we might have been
"unwise enough to commit, he availed himself of this aid, because, by
"so doing, he rid himself of the necessity of minutely quoting at what
"precise time, under what circumstances, and in what manner this
"important document had originally been composed. He undoubt-
"edly thought such silence would lead to premises which would
"exonerate him, and compromise the Imperial Government of France
"instead.

"Such a proceeding need not be further commented upon; suffice
"it to publish it, and all Europe will be able to decide.

"Accept the assurance, etc., etc.,

"V. BENEDETTI."

The Parisian journals have exposed the flatness and shallowness of the aforesaid epistle, and emphatically avowed the absurdity of the supposition that Count Bismarck should have retained the manuscript for the purpose of handing it over to the King, after it had just before been said, and clearly demonstrated, that the manuscript contained the full expression of the ideas of Count von Bismarck. Had that been the case, of what use would have been the manuscript? Why! all Count Bismarck had to do was to verbally communicate to the King his ideas, which certainly would have been done more impressively than with a document composed by the French Ambassador.

To an equal certainty the Parisians comprehended from Benedetti's letter the inadequateness of the rejection of the accusation, so that shortly afterwards a circular appeared of the Duke of Grammont's to the French diplomatic body abroad, which was intended to serve as an answer to the accusations of Count Bismarck in his last circular, and neutralize its effect. The French circular said:

PARIS, the 3d August, 1870.

Y. Exc.: We have, this day, become acquainted with the further meaning of the telegram which Count Bismarck has transmitted to the Prussian Ambassador in London, in order to communicate to England those supposed secrets, of which the Chancellor of the North German Union professes to be aware. His dispatch, however, contains no additional and essentially important information beyond the facts which he has already brought to light. We, ourselves, find only some more improbabilities. Public opinion has already pronounced judgment upon these assertions, which do not gain authority by the boldness with which they are repeated. We consider it as finally settled, in spite of all denial, that the Emperor Napoleon never proposed to Prussia a treaty which had for its purpose the forcible annexation of Belgium. This idea belongs exclusively to Bismarck, and intended to serve him as one of the means with which to manage his unscrupulous policy, which, however, is now as we hope fast approaching its frustration. I would have altogether refrained from reciting assertions, the wrongfulness of which stands to-day manifested, if the author of the Prussian dispatch, with a want of tact which has no precedent to my knowledge in any diplomatic document, had not cited relatives of the Emperor as having been the bearers of such compromising communications and messages. With what a disgust I feel necessitated to follow and keep an eye upon the Prussian Chancellor, and pursue a course contrary to my habits, I cannot tell; yet, I must overcome this feeling, because it is my duty to defend the members of the Imperial family against the horrid insinuations which are meant for them, and evidently directed to reach the Emperor himself.

It was at Berlin where Count Bismarck, taking hold of the initiation of the ideas, the first conception of which he to-day dexterously ascribes to us, accosted the French Prince, whom he now draws with contempt of all conventional rules into the circle of his polemic, with these words : You searched for "a thing impossible. You " want to take the provinces of the Rhine, which are German. Why " do you not rather annex Belgium ? made up of people partially of " your own race, who profess the same religion, and who speak the " same vernacular. The same thing I have already given the Emperor " to understand : that if he should share my views, we would aid " him to take Belgium. As far as I am concerned, if I was master " here, and not hindered by the stubbornness of the King, it would " have been done by this time." These words of the Prussian Chancellor were, so to say, repeated verbatim by Count von der Goltz, at the French Court. This very Ambassador made it so little a secret there that the number of witnesses who have heard it is considerable. I have to add that, at the time of the great exhibition, these propositions from Prussia reached the ears of a somewhat more than exalted personage who took a precise notice of it, and even now remembers it well. Besides it was with Count Bismarck no effervescent whim; on the contrary, a well meditated project which he fostered with his ambitious plans, and in which he persevered with a pertinacity which augured realization until it was wrecked upon the unshakable will of the Emperor, whom he often visited in Paris, as well as in Biarritz and other places for that very purpose, but who declined to participate in a policy which was unworthy of Napoleon's loyalty.

I now quit this topic, which I have touched upon for the last time, being determined not to return to it any more, and approach a really new one, found in the dispatch of Count von Bismarck : "I have " reason to believe (so he says) that, if the treaty had not been made " public, France would have made us the offer after we had both "armed, to execute her propositions previously made, as we had now " together a well equipped army of more than a million of men, '' against unarmed Europe, by which Bismarck intended to convey: " to grant peace before or after the first battle, according to the pro- " posals of Mr. Benedetti, and of course at the expense of Belgium."

It would not be proper for the Government of the Emperor to suffer to consider such an assurance. In the face of Europe the Ministers of His I. Majesty demanded of Count Bismarck to produce a solitary proof from which it might be inferred they had shown an intention, either directly or indirectly, officially, or with aid of secret agents, to unite with Prussia for the purpose of committing an attentat upon the independance of Belgium similar to the one that has been enacted upon Hanover. We have not negotiated with Count von Bismarck either in regard to Belgium nor in regard to anything else. Far from seeking war, of which we stand accused, we have even requested Lord Clarendon to intervene with the Prussian Minister, in order to bring about a reciprocated disarmament, which important mission Lord Clarendon unhesitatingly undertook, out of friendship to France, as well as out of devotion to the ideas of peace.

But the following letter will prove to a fault that the ire of the French arose from the designs of their intervention, in 1866, having being frustrated by the victories of Sadowa and Konigsgratz, as France had but one motive by that intervention, if possibly to participate in the spoils without having done anything in the way of help of action. Of course, Germany never listened to it, and Bismarck paid nothing in the way of inches of territory.

Drouyn de l'Huys wrote to the Prussian Ambassador in Paris, Count v. d. Goltz :

VICHY, 3d August, 1866.

MY DEAR AMBASSADOR : I hasten to answer your letter of the day before yesterday, in regard to the wish of Count von Bismarck, that we (France) officially acknowledge the annexations which Prussia intends to make in Northern Germany.

As often as I have touched, in my conversations with you, upon this question of territorial modifications in favor of Prussia, I have expressed to you my confidence in the Berlin Cabinet, acknowledging the propriety and equity of France of asking a recompensation for it in a manner which shall have for its purpose the somewhat comparative increase of the defensive strength of the French Empire.

Of this sort of condition I reminded Count Benedetti, on the twenty-third of July, in a dispatch approved of by the Emperor. It was by him confidentially communicated to Count Bismarck, who acknowledging the pardonable nature of the principle, exchanged with him some ideas in regard to the manner and means by which the conception might be practically realized.

Said conversation, of which Count Bismarck told me in his letter of the twenty-sixth of July, preceded the signing of the preliminaries of peace, and of the armistice. It should be taken up again later. On the twenty-ninth, by telegram, in my answer to his letter, approved of by the Emperor, I have precisely stated our views. Our Ambassador must have received the telegram either at Nickolsburg or in Berlin.

As you, my dear Count, refer in your letter to the conversations which you have had with the Emperor upon the subject, I have handed the letter to his Majesty, and requested his commands. Here is the answer which I am authorized to give you :

"When the Emperor offered his good services because of the recon-
"struction of peace, he did not hesitate to acknowledge that Prussia,
"by her victories, had a right to ask of Austria a territorial extension
"of her boundaries, to the figure of three to four millions of inhabit-
"ants upon it. If otherwise, the Emperor would not mistake that
"an undue enlargement would derange the equlibrium of strength
"upon our boundary.

"But His Majesty would not increase the difficulty of an affair which
"was of a general European magnitude, by treating beforehand with
"Prussia upon territorial questions which concern France particularly,
"besides were not mentioned in the preliminaries of peace.

"It appeared to his Majesty as enough to have alluded to this ques-
"tion, reserving to himself an examination of the same in unison with
"the Cabinet of Berlin, as soon as the role he had played as inter-
"ventor should have been finished.

"With these views upon the subject, the Emperor commanded me
"to instruct Count Benedetti as mentioned."

As soon as we shall have received his reply, I shall be enabled to inform you, my dear Count, of the decision of the Emperor in regard to the points comprising the contents of your letter.

D. DE L'H.

The manner in which these sly importunities of France were answered in Berlin, the diplomatic archives published last year have shown. It is certain that both Germany and France distrusted each other from those dates of Sadowa and Konigsgratz. It was nothing more nor less than a grudge.

It is well the heart is relieved, the pachydermal fury evaporated, and calm reason prevails.

Here follow the words which Count Daru, in a letter of the first of February, expressed to the Marquis of Lavalette, French Ambassador in London, as being the intentions of the French Government:

"I would assuredly not mix myself up in this affair, nor request of
"England to meddle with it, if it was merely and simply a banale and
"formal controversy, having no other purpose, than to afford Count
"Bismarck an opportunity of renewing his expression of a refusal.
"But it requires a firm, earnest, and positive action. The Secretary
"of State appears to predict that Count von Bismarck will experience
"a sensation of discontent and annoyance. It is possible, but not
"certain. In this expectation, however, it is perhaps well to so
"arrange matters that a negative answer is thereto at once avoided. I
"am convinced that reflection and time will bring the Chancellor to
"seriously contemplate the step England has taken; if he has not

" the first day refused explanation, then the interests of Prussia and
" Germany will soon loudly demand of him to relent. He will not
" arouse public opinion of the whole country against him. What,
" indeed, would be his position if we took away from him the sole
" pretext behind which he could possibly barricade himself, viz., the
" arming of France ?"

Upon this Count Bismarck answered he could not well do it and lay before the King the communication from the British Government, being sufficiently informed of the views of his Sovereign, as not to be able to anticipate the impression such communication would certainly make upon him. King William, he said, would observe in a step of that sort from the British Cabinet, a proof of a change in the friendly sentiments of England towards Prussia. Finally, the Chancellor recapitulated his explanation: "It would be impossible for Prussia
" to modify a military system which was firmly interwoven with the
" traditions of the country, formed a part of the basis of its consti-
" tution and was totally normal." Count Daru was not discomfited by this first response. On the 13th of February he wrote to Mr. von Lavalette: " I hope Lord Clarendon does not consider himself van-
" quished, and will lose his presence of mind. We shall very soon
" afford him another opportunity to return to the same attack when-
" ever he shall see fit to reopen the discourse upon the same topic
" with the German Chancellor, which has thus been interrupted.
" Our intention really is to diminish our contingent; we would have
" diminished it much more if we had received from the Chancellor of
" the North German Union a favorable answer; we shall now dimin-
" ish it less, because his answer was negative; nevertheless, we do
" diminish it, and the reduction I hope will amount to 10,000 men,
" each contingent; this number I shall propose. In this manner we
" shall attest our policy and intention by action, which are always
" worth more than words. Nine contingents diminished, each of
" 10,000 men, make a total of 90,000 men. That is something—a
" tenth of the army; I regret only that I cannot do more. The law in
" regard to the contingent shall soon be presented; Lord Clarendon
" may then judge whether it is time to remonstrate with Count Bis-
" marck, that it is the Prussian Government alone in Europe which
" does not make concession in favor of peace, and that it puts itself
" in a critical position among the nations of Europe, because it lends
" arms to all the world against itself, even against the people thus
" oppressed by military taxes as necessarily levied upon them.

Lively pressed, Count Bismarck considered it necessary to give Lord Clarendon new explanations. These were full of reticencies as transmitted to us by letter from Mr. von Lavalette, dated February 23d. The Chancellor of the North German Union had returned to his first resolution, and had had a conversation with King William upon the proposal as recommended by England. The King, however, had declined. Count Bismark based this refusal upon the apprehension of a possible French alliance between Austria and South Germany, and the inclination which France might evince in enlarging her boundary. Above all, he clouded his argument into the anxiety which the policy of Russia gave him, and upon this occasion made some pointed remarks in regard to the Court of St. Petersburg, which were incomprehensible to me.

These are the grounds upon which Count Bismarck based his non-compliance with the request of the French Imperial Government, as transmitted through Lord Clarendon, and duly represented as a loyal and conscientious matter.

If, therefore, Europe remained under arm when a million of men were about to wound each other upon battle-fields, then it is not any longer permissible to deny that Prussia is responsible for such a condition of things; she has rejected every thought in regard to disarmament when we have had the proposition made, and commenced by giving an example. Is not, moreover, this behavior explainable from the fact that in the same hour in which France diminished her contingent, the Prussian Cabinet organized in the dark the provoking candidature of a Prussian Prince for the Spanish Throne? No matter what calumnies the Chancellor of the North German Union may have invented, we are without fear. He has lost the right to find credence. The conscience of Europe and history shall say that Prussia provoked the present war by aiming an insult at France, while the latter was busy perfecting its political improvements, which affront no proud and courageous nation could have stood without deserving execration from all the world.

With assurances of high regard, etc., etc.,
(Signed) GRAMMONT.

Even the aforesaid circular was not sufficient to allay the distrust once aroused among the European Courts, as it contained nothing new beyond what Benedetti had already advanced by stating, without proofs, that Count Bismarck had been the originator of the project which the Emperor of the French had perseveringly rejected. The most interesting part of the document is, however, the manner in which developments, as systematically arranged by Count Bismarck, were made to connect with the candidature of the Prince of Hohenzollern for the throne of Spain, its conception likewise ascribed to him and which fusion had to serve France to get as a pretext for the inauguration of the present war. By this artful device the Duke of Grammont is lucky enough to put down Count Bismarck as the abominable originator of the war, and place France near him as the innocent lamb which had to go against its will, that civilization might be saved and the disturbed balance of power in Europe readjusted. It cannot be denied, though, that the following document, which had appeared not long before the one just given, and serving as an introductory to the same, has been executed with so much dramatic skill, that it is not to be wondered at that in the eyes of Frenchmen, who love and admire, above everything, a good theatrical effect, it appeared as an expression of the most verified truth. This document reads as follows:

Paris, 21 July, 1870.

Gentlemen:—You are already aware of the entanglement of facts which have brought about the breach of peace with Prussia. The announcement which the Government of the Emperor had, on the 15th inst., issued forth from the tribunal of the corporation of great nations, the exact contents of it I have duly communicated to you, has explained to France and Europe the quick changes wrought in a negotiation which had for its purpose the preservation of peace, during the management of which the secret plans of an adversary, determined to contract our exertions in behalf of peace, developed themselves, and at the same ratio at which we redoubled our efforts of securing it.

Be it that the Berlin Cabinet considered war necessary in order to be enabled of carrying out its old plans against the independence of the German States, be it that the Berlin Cabinet was not content with possessing, in the very heart of Europe, a military power which had already become extremely formidable to its neighbors, and was anxious of making use of that power, self-evidently for the purpose of deranging the international balance of power in Europe, at any rate the well defined intention to refuse a positively necessary guarantee for our security as well as our honor, clearly shows itself throughout its demeanor.

The following was undoubtedly the plan projected against us: According to an agreement made with non-responsible persons, it should have carried the result of the measure directly to the spot, where the Cortes were to be suddenly made acquainted with the candidature of the Prussian Prince. A vote thus attained by surprise and forestalling the mature deliberation of the Spanish people upon so important an event, should then — such was the hope — unanimously proclaim Prince Leopold von Hohenzollern the Heir to the Scepter of Charles V.

" In this manner Europe would have found itself confronted by an
" accomplished fact, while it indulged in speculations upon our con-
" stant readiness to advance the grand principle of the sovereignty of

"peoples. Therefore, Europe expected that France would stand
"firmly by that principle in spite of her transient anger, when brought
"opposite the expression of a nation apparently real, for whom all
"the world is aware of our sympathies.

"As soon as it had been informed of the danger, this Government
"did not hesitate to inform the agents of the country, as well as all
"the European Cabinets, of it; to then counteract the manœuvre, we
"were assisted in by public opinion, which became the legitimate ally
"of the Government. The impartial minds have nowhere been dis-
"appointed in regard to the real state of things, these quickly compre-
"hended that if it touched us painfully to see Spain assigned to play-
"ing a role in the exclusive interest of an ambitious dynasty, not at
"all suitable to the loyalty of that chivalrous people, besides did so
"little accord with the promptings and transfer of friendship which
"binds Spain to us, we could not be expected to dissemble our
"constant esteem for the independence of her national decisions.

"One has felt it that the but little scrupulous policy of the Prus-
"sian Government played here its part. That Government is it in
"reality, which, not considering itself bound by common right and
"regard of the rules, to which the wisest powers have possessed the
"wisdom of bowing, has attempted to burden a deceived Europe with
"so dangerous an extension of its influence. France, however, has
"taken the case of the balance of power in hand, viz: The case of
"all nations which are jeopardized by a disproportioned enlargement
"of some kingly house.

"Every nation, we take a pleasure in so saying, is mistress of its
"own destiny. This principle, which France has openly acknowl-
"edged, has become one of the main laws of modern politics. But
"the right of each nation, exactly the same as the right of every in-
"dividual, is kept in check by the right of another, and it is forbid-
"den to a nation, under pretext of exercising its own right of sover-
"eignty, to endanger the existence or the security of a neighboring
"one. In this sense spoke one of our great orators, Mr. von Lam-
"artine, in 1847: that the moment the question comprised the election
"of a sovereign, a government had never the right to demonstrate
"demands, but it had the right to remonstrate them. This doctrine
"is under circumstances adhered to by all cabinets, and is analogous
"to the one in which the candidature of the Prince of Hohenzollern
"has put us, and particularly to the one of the year 1831, to the one
"in the Belgian question of 1830 and in the Greek question of 1862.
"In the Belgian question the voice of all Europe was heard. The
"five great powers decided. The three Courts which took the Greek
"question in hand were unanimous among themselves, being guided

"by interests which they had in common with each other, not to
"accept the throne of Greece for one of their princes.

"The Cabinets of Paris, London, Vienna, Berlin and St. Peters-
"burg, all of which were represented at the London Conference,
"made an example of it; they set it down as a rule, when negotiating
"on questions affecting the peace of the world. They did homage—
"so solemnly—to this great law for the equilibrium of strength, as
"forming the basis of the European political system. In vain the
"Belgian National Congress insisted, in spite of this agreement, to
"elect the Duke of Nemours; France adhered to its obligation and
"rejected the crown, which the Belgian delegates had brought to
"Paris. But France insisted in a like manner that the candidature
"of the Duke of Leuchtenberg should similarly not be accepted.
"Likewise in Greece, the Government of France prevented the can-
"didature of Prince Alfred of England, and of another candidate,
"the Duke of Leuchtenberg.

"England, acknowledging the weight of our proposition, declared
"at Athens that the Queen had forbidden her son to accept the Crown
"of Greece. Russia declared similarly in regard to the Duke of
"Leuchtenberg; besides, that nobleman does not come within the
"pedigree of the Imperial family. Finally, and voluntarily, the
"Emperor Napoleon declared his adhesion to these principles, and
"published a note, on the first of September, 1860, in the *Moniteur*,
"in which he refused the candidature of Prince Murat for the throne
"of Naples. Prussia, which we had not omitted of reminding of
"these precedents, appeared for a moment to yield to our represen-
"tation; Prince Leopold declined the candidature; one was flattered
"that peace would not be disturbed. But this hope soon waned.
"New anxieties arose, which increased to a certainty, that Prussia,
"without seriously withdrawing her pretensions, contemplated to
"gain time. The language upon the subject, as made use of by the
"head of the family of Hohenzollern—first evasive, then decisive and
"haughty—his refusal to adhere to the same avowed non-acceptance
"in future, the treatment of our *Charge d'Affaires*, who had been
"denied further audiences, disabling him from amicably arrang-
"ing this case as instructed, finally the publicity to which these
"extraordinary preliminaries were exposed to in the Prussian news-
"papers, and which had been given of the same to the various Cabi-
"nets—all these consecutive symptoms of hostile plans could not but
"put aside every doubt in minds the most partially inclined. Is there
"a mistake possible, when a Sovereign, who can dispose of over a mil-
"lion of soldiers, and putting his hand upon his sword, declares he
"will reserve to himself his decision, and be guided by circumstances
"only? We have about arrived at the utmost point, where a nation

"which feels what it owes to itself does not further negotiate for
"demands upon its own honor. If these last named proofs in this
"woeful controversy do not throw a sufficient light upon the matured
"plans of the Berlin Cabinet, a circumstance will certainly do it, which
"is far less known, but which, nevertheless, stamps those plans as
"real and decisive.

"The fact is, the thought to put a prince of Hohenzollern upon the
"throne of Spain was not a new one. Already, in March, 1869, we
"had been given to understand, by our *Charge d'Affaires* at Berlin, that
"such a thought existed. We authorized him to explain to Count
"Bismarck how we, the Imperial Government, would view such
"eventuality. Count Benedetti had made it known in several conver-
"sations which he had upon the subject with the Chancellor of the
"North German Union, as well as with the Under Secretary of State,
"that we could not permit it that a Prussian prince should succeed in
"reigning on the other side of the Pyrenees.

"Count Bismarck on his part declared that we had it not necessary
"to busy ourselves with a combination which he himself considered
"inexecutable; and later, at a time when the Chancellor happened to be
"absent, and Count Benedetti thought it a good moment to express
"himself unbelievingly and pressingly, Mr. Von Thiele had given his
"word of honor that the Prince of Hohenzollern was not in earnest a
"candidate for the Spanish throne, nor could he become one.

"If one should draw into doubt the veracity and truthfulness of
"such explicit official assurances, all diplomatic intercourse would
"cease to be the pledge of European peace, and be nothing but a
"snare and a danger. As soon as our *Charge d'Affaires* communi-
"cated those declarations to us without reserve, the Imperial Gov-
"ernment considered itself as notified to interpret the same favorably.
"It has been constrained to draw into doubt the good belief of this
"assurance up to the moment when this combination suddenly
"revealed itself, which evidently is the contrary to the same. Unex-
"pectedly retiring from the word given to us, without even the at-
"tempt to release herself from an obligation, Prussia has prepared for
"us a real disappointment. Informed of the value which the most
"formal assurances of Prussian statesmen possess, we considered it a
"peremptory duty in future incumbent upon us, of asking a guarantee
"for our honesty, which should secure us against a new attempt of
"disrespect. We therefore were obliged to do as we have done, viz.,
"to insist upon receiving a security which should be definitive and
"earnest, and not full of reserves, as the former.

"It is evident that the Court of Berlin bears the responsibility for
"the war from a time previous to the combination, while it had all

"the means at its disposal of avoiding it, but insisted upon having.
"And under what circumstances has it sought the strife?

"After France had, during four years, given proofs of an unalter-
"able moderation,—after she had abstained with an anxiety perhaps
"carried too far from reminding the Prussian Government of the
"treaties which had been made by intervention of the Emperor, the
"international disregard discernible in all the acts of said Govern-
"ment clearly demonstrates that it already intended to rid itself of the
"same when it signed the contract.

"Europe bears witness to our conduct, and has had time to com-
"pare that of Prussia. To-day it may pronounce its veto on the jus-
"tice of our cause. Whatever may be the fate of battles, we expect,
"without disquietude, the judgment of contemporaries, as well as that
"of the future.

"Pray accept the assurance of, etc., etc.;
"GRAMMONT."

This remarkable document, the sophistry and illusive surmises as to consequence of the contents of which an unpreposessed mind can easily grasp, was vigorously reinforced by two proclamations which were no less noticeable, one of which was directed to the French people. I shall here produce and comment upon both. The procla- mation to the French people reads as follows :

"There are, during the existence of a nation, solemn moments :
"when the honor of a nation, violently assailed, rises, with an irre-
"sistable might, when it commands all other interests, and manages
"alone and directly the fate of the nation. One of those decisive
"moments is the present one for France. Prussia, which we have
"shown the most forgiving sentiments to during the war of 1866, has
"ever since taken no notice at all of our good will and forbear-
"ance. Impetuously pursuing its course of conquests it has given
"reasons for mistrustfulness; made everywhere excessive armaments
"necessary; transforming Europe into a military camp, in which
"apprehension prevails.

"The glorious flag which we once more unfurl to those who pro-
"vokes us, is the same which has carried the civilizing ideas of our
"great revolution all over Europe ; it represents the same ideas ; it
"will inspire the same feelings of devotion. Frenchmen, I am ready
"to place myself at the head of this brave army, which is imbued
"with a keen sense of duty, and animated by its love of France; the
"army knows its own worth, for it has seen how, in four divisions of
"the globe, victory accompanied its footsteps. I take my son with
"me, notwithstanding his youthfulness he understands the duties
"which his name demands of him ; he is proud of being permitted
"to share the dangers of those who fight for France. A last inter-

"vening event has been added, which brings more fully to light the
"changeableness of international relations, showing the full earnest-
"ness of the situation. Opposite the new pretensions of Prussia are
"our reinforcements. One has despised them, followed by a testi-
"fied contempt. Our country has been deeply incensed in conse-
"quence, and the war-cry heard from one end of France to the other.
"Nothing is now left to us but to let our fate be decided by force of
"arms. We do not wage war against Germany, the independence of
"which we respect. We have the wish that the people of whom the
"German Union is composed may, of their own free will, decide in
"this case. We ourselves require a state of things which guarantees
"our security and our future. We want to attain to a lasting peace.
"God will bless our exertions. A great people defending a just cause
"are invincible.

"NAPOLEON."

It is interesting to observe how groundless reproaches against Prussia, over-estimation of their own actions, and general egotism are harmoniously blended together for the purpose of producing a semblance of a substance, palatable to French military vanity. In regard to the praised forbearance of France we now find out its source: the hope of enlarging her territory; the "victories in four divisions of "the globe." It might be useful to remember that Napoleon III did not obtain one without allies; as soon as he fought alone he did not achieve anything, which the events in Mexico have clearly shown, and this present war still more so. How little correct the assurance is that the war-cry was heard from one end of France to the other, is best attested by the demands for peace from Nizza and Bordeaux, and by the remarks from Michelet and Louis Blanc in newspapers. Those of Louis Blanc may serve as an example.

He wrote to the *Rappel:* " . . . . Be it well understood that this
"war to which we are driven by the martial spirit of honest minds,
"betrayed by the martial spirit of knavish souls, is entered into on
"the one side to make despotism stronger than liberty, and on the
"other side to cover the lack of success of a Napoleonic dynasty and
"adjust the damage done at the expense of France. A double reason
"to be on guard and to prevent it! The Union of Germany is, nev-
"ertheless, a danger. I repeat, that this Union, difficult and slow
"as it can be effected in times of peace, will instantly be consolidated
"when the war trumpet sounds. Put Germany under threats of war,
"one may rely on it—she will rise to a man. Don't speak any more
"of annihilating Prussia, but reflect upon annihilating Germany. A
"terrible shock, that of the Latin and Germanic races, a shock in
"which we, a Latin nation, would, strange to say, have Latin nations

" arraigned against us—a shock which would sow enmities for ever,
" and carry civilization back a century, perhaps two. That it is which
" is demanded of France, to that she shall allow herself to be driven,
" under the pretext that the vanity of some diplomatist is tanta-
" mount to the dignity of the nation; and for what purpose? it is
" barely concealed; of giving the baptismal of glory to the supposed
" heir to the throne! Great people of France! is it possible that one
" dares to count upon a harrassed mind to such an extent? dares to
" ensnare your bravery to such a degree?"

The language of many others in the newspapers conveys pretty much the same meaning, as the words of Louis Blanc, demanding peace in the most determined manner, and shows the power of republicanism.

Finally, the reproaches against Prussia of her desire for conquest, her insatiable ambition, etc., etc., those are as old and unfounded as they are unproved, and if she is particularly reproached because of having lately enlarged her territory, it is not to be forgotten that Prussia was menaced in her very existence, during the war with Austria, by the hostility of Hanover and other States, and the artful devises of jealous adversaries, among whom France was by no means the smallest one. Besides, Prussia had been previously put at the Congress of 1815, in a position, the natural condition and doubtfulness of which, was such as to sooner or later predict a rupture or a radical change in the destiny of Prussia, lest she should have had to rue complete annihilation.

Herein consisted the impetus, germinating the power, which, since 1815 has produced all these events, and which is not to be attributed to vainglorious ambition, or a desire for conquest, which the world has been made to fancifully believe as having alone actuated the policy of Prussia, but to self-preservation through self-defense and the true belief in God and themselves.

The second document commences with the same words as the first, so that it might be inferred it has had the same author, it is by no means less noticeable than the first, and reads as follows:

" There are during the existence of a nation solemn moments when
" God affords them an opportunity of showing who they are, and
" what they can do. One of those moments has come for France!
" One has often had the opinion that the great nation, so resolute in
" attack, did not well know how to bear misfortune. What now
" developes itself before our eyes resents the calumny with falsity.
" The bearing of the population shows no discouragement; on the con-
" trary, a patriotic fierceness towards the aggressors of France, who
" shall here find their graves. All Frenchmen shall rise to a man. They
" will remember their ancestors and think of those who shall follow.
" Behind them centuries of glory, before them a future full of liberty

" and power, which their heroism shall create. Never before has
" France shown her noble pride and the strength of her national
" character in such an equally great and imposing manner. Every-
" body full of enthusiasm exclaims: To arms! to conquer or die! While
" our soldiers heroically defend the soil of the country, *Europe is
" justly full of anxiety in regard to the successes of Prussia. One does
" not know how far the ambition of that insatiable power may carry it,
" should a final triumph make it still more presumptive.*

" It is an unchangeable law of history that every nation which dis-
" turbs the general balance of power by its extraordinary success, is
" awakening a reaction consequent upon those very victories, and cre-
" ates for itself the enmity of all other nations. It cannot fail that
" this truth shall now again be confirmed by facts. So especially con-
" sidered.

" *Who, then, after all, is interested in a reconstruction of a German
" Empire?* Who, after all, can wish that the North Sea and the
" Baltic become Prussian lakes? Is it, perhaps, *Sweden, Norway, and
" Denmark*, which the triumph of Prussia would annihilate? or is it
" *Russia*, whose interest it is, more than any other power, to protect
" the equilibrium of the North against the advance of a compact Ger-
" many? Is it, perhaps, *England*, which as a great naval power and
" protector of Denmark, is obliged to protest against further pro-
" gress in the formation of the Prussian marine? Is it, perhaps, *Hol-
" land*, which has been long enough threatened by the intrigues of
" Bismarck?

" In regard to Austria, the reconstruction of the German Empire
" by the house of Hohenzollern, would be the most dangerous blow
" dealt not only to the dynasty of the Hapsburgs, but to the very
" existence of an Austro-Hungarian monarchy. Prussia would surely
" endeavor to make promises to the Cabinet of Vienna, but one knows
" what belief to attach to the words of Bismarck. A proffered guaran-
" tee, of whatever nature, could never be stronger than the ties which
" have bound Prussia to the former German Union, and, notwith-
" standing which, Prussia, unmindful of her obligations, has rented in
" such a violent manner. A definitive triumph of the house of Hohen-
" zollern would be for Italy no less deplorable than for Austria. A
" German Empire would seek to provide for itself, at all costs,
" countries bordering upon the sea, as well in the South as in the
" North. It would covet possession of Venice, Triest, as well as Am-
" sterdam. Thus, the regeneration of Italy would be in danger, as
" well as Austria and Holland.

" We appeal to the Governments and the nations of Europe to tear
" Europe off the grasp of Prussian despotism, in order that they
" may be able to assist us, by alliances and sympathies, to protect the

"European balance of power. In England, Denmark, and Sweden
"there are already signs of such a turn. Austria and Italy have com-
"menced to arm. Our patriotism is proof against all dangers. The
"more seriously the circumstances, the greater the energy the nation
"shall display."

That what especially rivets the attention of the aforesaid document is not the *passus*, which places Prussia as an insatiably ambitious power in Europe, which should be fully feared, and which accusation serves but as a somewhat modified repetition of what had been advanced in the previous document ; but the *passus* in which the question is put and answered—who it is that after all is interested in the restoration of a German Empire ? The answer, of course, is: "nobody."

On the contrary, all are interested that such a consolidation should not be realized ; in other words, that Germany should remain weak and disunited as in times of yore. One has denominated this *passus* in diplomatic circles : a mendicancy of France to obtain alliances, and justly so ; for that is its version from the one side. But the purpose of it is by no means thereby exhausted. On the contrary, the more important and extensively versified portion of that *passus* has not therein even been touched. This *passus* expresses on the one side the apprehension of France of a change in affairs as inaugurated previously to 1864, and which the *Moniteur* calls "normal," viz., predicting the destruction of the supremacy of France presumptively exercised over the European continent ever since the days of Louis XIV, and of the possibility of a future cessation of the supremacy of England in the European waters through the full development of the strength of Germany. The "*enteinte cordiale*" between France and Great Britain, of which so much was made, rested in its exact meaning upon the thoughts to strengthen by mutual action the supremacy of both in Europe, for the purpose of keeping it at bay, for the execution of which strategy it became, however, absolutely necessary that Germany remained disunited, and consequently weak and powerless.

This "*enteinte cordiale*" cooled off when Great Britain thought it detected other purposes on the part of France, which were directed towards absorbing from England, at a fit opportunity, her share of the supremacy at sea, which thought matured in English opinion by France constantly strengthening her fortifications at Cherbourg, besides noticing the considerable increase of her navy, as there was no other nation in Europe but England against which such hostile preparations of magnitude might be warranted to be so developed in embryo. The pointed hints which Napoleon III threw out with reference to and in anticipation of a successful realization of the assiduous and indefatigable exertions of Prussia striving to form a German Empire, should serve to stimulate the commercial ambition as well as awaken the suspicion of Great Britain. Of course, his purpose was to again attract that great moral power to the modern alliance, so as to cosily hide his mischievous connivings before the world. How, in 1855, so shortly after his ascension to the throne as a revenging spectre of his uncle, he ever succeeded in duping England to such an extent as to induce that stern power to completely untomb at St. Helena the shade of Napoleon I, in the eyes of the Holy alliance, is more than history will ever draw information of and fathom from blue books.

Similar purposes should the addresses serve, which Napoleon transmitted to the other nations of Europe, as mentioned in the aforesaid document, leaving nothing further to remark but that those were of as feeble a nature as they were frivolous. He simply relied on the feeling of awe, which pervaded all Europe, and which the wars of his uncle had bequeathed to him as a very serviceable legacy. The French nation forsaking in 1848, the Republic, relied upon the talisman of the name Napoleon as creating a reality, expecting nothing short of a repetition of a victorious run through Europe. The battle of Sadowa, therefore, ignited the martial spirit of the French, and throwing themselves upon Napoleon, forced him to the mad attempt of this war. It shows that the world never went beyond antecedents, and with Indian fierceness and ignorance failed to consider that the foe of barbarity, the A B C book, had been about and at work. Naturally they all have found it out by this time, that the combined warlike hordes of the world could not now conquer Germany, monarchical though she yet is, having but lately been freed from political shackles, which of course prevented her of doing the republic.

The same school-book will affix itself to the bravest soldier holding fire-arms in self-defense, as David slew Goliah, strip wars of their glory by the scientific process of extermination and additional moral courage, until all mankind shall disarm and live law-abidingly, peacefully and happily.

As many proofs more could be shown and defended in favor of an accomplishment of the endeavor to form a strong German empire, and that such a power could not but exercise a beneficial influence upon the peace and liberty of Europe. In fact, Germany owes her present success to her clear-headedness which defines to her the duty of absorbing upon civilized grounds of humanity and charitableness, all other strayed-off German elements, monarchical alienated, besides Alsace and Lorraine in due avail of her physical powers if made reasonably necessary.

As it is this enlightened feeling which pervades her actions in this war, not a feudal delight to cripple her adversary, she will not discontinue uniting the remainder of Germanic races at once. She has been signally crowned with immediate success in this war, at the same time ridding herself and Europe of the glare of igneous firebrands of war in a feudal sense.

She will now continue in a friendly manner to first induce Austria and Russia to act humanely just, and give up the Germans and not thwart the happiness of millions of people now forlorn and alien.

The land which said aliens at present occupy, shall by Germany be most liberally bought and paid for.

Speedily accomplished either way, peaceably or by main force, she shall have received twofold blessings; the exquisiteness of conscience, of having performed her duty to the fatherland, and the impossibility of a re-occurrence of war, especially with France, should the master spirit of faith be there once more overruled, and the republic be a third time made a sham, which republic alone places France to-day next to the United States of America in general importance of the civilization of the world, attained so far. The republic shall eventually intimately befriend France with Germany, if the latter country continues to prove its wisdom by at all times of the future assisting the French people in never permitting a monarch to again rule over France, plunge the world into agony and the French nation into moral and political retrogradation.

Secondly, and especially important, is the document, because it expresses the leading opinions of all the European nations in regard to the Union of Germany, as so considered at least by France. It is a French opinion, from a party stand-point, therefore one-sided, notwithstanding there is much truth in it worth noticing and to be reflected upon.

Thirdly, and finally, the document points out the means of which Napoleon III availed himself in order to attain to his end with the nations he has mentioned; they consisted of suspicion, an awakening distrust and general mischievous talk of results already gained, or to be so nearly. As a set-off to such damaging insinuations, one may simply remember the conduct of the European nations, as shown throughout this matter, in order to realize the weak ground from which the wrongfulness of French insinuations had been produced.

The trouble is that France, with but thirty-six millions of population and no more, feels that she has far less population than a United Germany has, comprising the Germanic race on the continent of Europe sure to unite ere very long. From nowhere has a voice been heard which justified the proceedings of France, or sanctioned the motives for the war. Everywhere Napoleon's manner has been most severely censured, and instead of having served him as a moral assistance, as he boasts of, it has been transferred to the Germans as provoked to war because attacked, and has been gladly accorded and avowed by all nations, with the exception of the Scandinavians, equally troubled as France, for the very same reasons of a minority of population, compared with the Union of the Germans.

Previously to the commencement of actual hostilities at the time when the German Diet was about to adjourn at Berlin, Count Bismarck entered and issued the following manifest:

" It has been my intention to lay before you the documents in con-
" secutive order, which are in the hands of the Government, and
" refer to the origin of the dispute with France. I expect these doc-
" uments every moment. For the present I have but to explain that
" the collection is very meagre. We have received in this whole
" affair but *one* official communication, and that is the declaration of
" war [motion]. That is the only official document which has at all
" been transmitted to us by the French Government. In regard to
" it, all conversation which Count Benedetti, in his capacity as *Charge*
" *d'Affaires*, had upon the subject with the King, privately and at the
" Springs of Ems:—
" Likewise all definitions which one has attempted to force in that
" way, and which, perhaps would have been so forced if His Majesty
" had been less manly and firm of character than he is, would always
" have been considered personal expressions which the Monarch would
" have confirmed in a different manner, if that had been his earnest
" will.

" After having said this in advance, I take the liberty of throwing a short glance at those other documents, which were produced after the affair could not any longer be peaceably arranged, simply to explain to the other Governments how this case developed itself. In the order here given, these communications contain the particular newspaper telegram already known, which the French Ministry consider as the real cause of the war, for the reason that one has attached to it the importance of a " note " by which the French Cabinet fancies itself to have been deceived. [Hear ! Hear !] I shall not go to the trouble of explaining what is meant by " notes." For all those at all acquainted with diplomacy it is enough to understand that " newspaper telegrams " cannot be qualified and become " notes." The gentlemen then have taken good care not to produce the said document, [Hear ! Hear !] for everything would have been considered as naught upon the contents of the document becoming known. The second and third documents are those already known through the newspapers, referring to the authenticated occurrences at Ems. Then, fourthly, a dispatch from Baron v. Werther, dated Paris, twelfth July. That one, at least, is an official document, exchanged between Prussian authorities, and not between Prussia and France. In this dispatch there are the contents given of a conversation which Barron v.

Werther had had with the French Minister of Foreign Affairs, and at the same time with the Minister of Justice, Monsieur Ollivier. In this dispatch we are made acquainted with the unacceptable demand of a letter of apology [Laughter] which the King should have to write. I have, hereupon, answered the *Charge d'Affaires* nothing more than that he could not but have misunderstood the wishes of the French Government, as they had appeared to me impossible. I do not consider myself justified to lay before the King—demands of that sort. [Bravo!] I wrote to the Representative he might ask of the French Government to put their demand in form, and to have it here officially presented through their *Charge d'Affaires*. The fifth is the circular of the eighteenth of July, and the sixth the dispatch from the English Government to intervene. The seventh is the response of the Chancellor of the North German Union, which has not as yet been made known to the House.

"Count Bismarck read the reply, from which it appears that although the proposition of an intervention had been gratefully acknowledged, and nothing would have been rejected which might have enhanced the security for an acceptable basis of peace, yet, one was now no longer in a position to avail oneself of the initiative, after having unofficially heard that France had already declined the intervention of England, because such a step would be misunderstood by the Germans, whose national pride had been wounded by the threats of France. The gentlemen might rest assured that the Foreign Office of the North German Union had not been one moment remiss in advising moderation and quiet.

"Upon this follows the French version of the declaration of war, of which the translation into German is already known, and then a circular to the Ambassadors of the North German Union, which explains the causes from which originated the war, and the manner in which we treat the affair. [Lively applause.] The documents shall, after the close of this session, be immediately handed over by the Chancellor of the North German Union to the President of the House, and then published in the daily papers."

Thereupon the session was declared closed by the President, and when afterwards resumed, Bismarck explained:

GENTLEMEN:—The three Presidents of the Diet have been permitted already, shortly after noon, to transmit to the King the addresses which had been decided upon this forenoon. His Majesty ordered the addresses to be read to him, and then directed us in his name to express to the House his most sincere and grateful thanks; for as the King literally said: "The beautiful and ennobling expressions of devotion to the German Fatherland." [Here the whole house rose.] In this declaration so unanimously decided upon, the King recognizes likewise a pledge for the final and complete success of the great tasks which lie before him and before us. He likewise found his full confidence confirmed that the nation would never cease to pursue those aforesaid tasks with unrelenting perseverance. [Lively applause.]

In order to more lucidly explain the declaration of the Diet, we may as well here produce the newspaper telegram, to which the Chancellor refers, and which the French Minister valued as a "note" and reasoned that therefrom had emanated the actual cause of the war.

"After the advices of the refusal of the hereditary Prince of
" Hohenzollern had been officially transmitted by the Spanish to the
" Imperial French Government, the French *Charge d'Affaires* had
" demanded of the King of Prussia, at Ems, that the King should
" authorize him to telegraph to Paris, that he pledged himself for all
" future not to give his sanction to such an alternative of acceptance,
" should a Prince of Hohenzollern again return to the candidature.
" The King hereupon declined to further receive the French *Charge*
" *d'Affaires*, and had sent him word through his Aid-de-camp on duty,
" that he had nothing further to communicate to him."

On the 21st of July the Chancellor again adjourned the Diet, because in one respect the purpose for its assembling had been realized, and in the other, the Government, in consequence of the pressure of events, had now to direct its attention to other more important matters, especially the necessary preparations for the war about to commence, the more obligatory as the time for their completion had been but tardily given. The most important point of all was, of course, the arming of the troops in the shortest possible time, which succeeded so happily and speedily, thanks to the admirable efficiency of the army organization, that it became impossible for the French to surprise the Germans.

PART THE THIRD.

THE PROVISIONAL BATTLE-GROUND.

The German-French Frontier is divided into two entirely distinct parts. From Basle in Switzerland, to Lanterburg, a distance of twenty-two and a half miles (one German mile is equal to four and a quarter English), the Rhine forms the frontier, while the Bavarian palatinate of the Rhine, and the Prussian province of the Rhine commence at Lauterburg to be the neighbors of France. The Rhine along its right —the German—bank, is accompanied as far as Lauterberg by the heavily timbered mountain ridges of the so-called "Black Forest." These stretch nearly down to the banks of the river, and continue so nearly down from Schlingen. From there mountains extend off the river at a distance of about one to two German miles, forming the fertile valley of the Rhine. The discontinuation of the Black Forest from these plains is quite abrupt and bluff. The Black Forest at the upper end, as far as the River Murg, appears as a rugged and almost impenetrable fastness, over the summit of which but few paths lead. Lengthways along the summit the mountain roads are almost impassable, so that the Black Forest there may be considered a heavy obstacle to all military operations. Its breadth from Muhlheim to Blumberg is ten German miles, although in the north it loses of its breadth as well as elevation, footing up but six and a half miles between Freiburg and Donau-Eschingen, and but six miles between Baden and the city of Weil, at an elevation the same as at the strong fortress Rastatt. The central part of the Black Forest, from the Murg to the Pfing, admits of a more passable formation, and at its lower end from the Pfing to the Neckar it gently verges into undulating hill lands. In consequence of which the central and lower sections of the Black Forest can barely be considered more than a weighty obstacle to military operations, when large armies are concerned. Further to the north is the Odenwald, or Odenforest, with which the space from the river Neckar to the river Main is filled. The slope of these hillocks are steep towards the Neckar, and even the more elevated portions of it are rough and densely timbered. The leading roads avoid the Odenwald ; others are scarce, and very bad in rainy weather and during winter, because of the limy and muddy soil, so that this hilly section might likewise be termed an obstacle to military operations. (Between the Rhine and the western section of the river Main, the Odenwald, as well as the Black Forest, afford the richest kind of farming lands to a width of two to three German miles.)

Upon the left bank of the Rhine, opposite the Black and the Oden Forests, stretch the Vosges mountains, upon French soil. These rise in the neighborhood of the source of the river Moselle (in equal elevation with Muhlheim, Blumberg, therefore exactly opposite the Black Forest in its largest horizontal and vertical extension) and like the Black Forest, fall steeply towards the valley of the Rhine, gradually diminishing towards the north, in both elevation and breadth. In the palatinate, as well as in the mountains of the Haardt, the Vosges border there upon a broad valley of the Rhine, and are frequently crossed by roads and even railroads.

If one so compares the so-called military sections of the country adjacent to both banks of the Rhine, one finds that the higher and less passable elevations of the mountains on both sides are in the South, and not easily suitable for military operations. From Rastatt-Hagenau down, the valley of the Rhine appears to become much broader, and the mountains more passable. Should, therefore, military operations take place south of the river Main, it must necessarily be between Mayence, Saarbruck, Strasburg, Rastatt, Pforzheim, Heilbronn, Wurzburg, and Frankfort-on-the-Main. The impassable parts of the mountains of the "Oden Forest" may be in this case avoided, from the southwest, either *via* Darmstadt or Heidelberg, towards Wurzburg. Up to Lauterburg, the Rhine opposite France, forms a line of defense. The German-French boundary from Lauterburg, as far as the neutral Grand Duchy of Luxemburg, however, is free, and the German territory behind exposed to hostile invasion. To the northwest, from Lauterbach, the Haardt rises, of which mountain chain already mention has been made. It falls abruptly towards the east, while towards the west it gradually verges into an open, hilly ground. From Kaisers Lautern, through a sort of sink which separates the Haardt from the Mountains of Donner, as well as through numerous valleys, there lead railroads and many other roads, from the upper Saar to the Rhine, as far as Lauterburg-Bingen. The valley of the Nahe forms towards the northwest, the last chance for these communications. On the other side of the Nahe, between it and the other rivers, the Moselle and the Saar, the Mountains of the Dog's Back extend, which, together with the Mountains of Taunus, surround the stream, and like those latter mountains, characterize themselves by their rocky ground and yawning abysses, encircling the lower valleys. Along the narrow valley of the Moselle, spirally appear, opposite the Dog's Back, the principal sections of the West Lower-Rhinish hilly landscapes, which cover the whole country half down the Maas, and are known by the names, Eifel and High Veen, together with the mountainous country of the Westerwald, (or Westerforest) and that of the so-called Sauerland encompassing the Rhine further down as far as the neighborhood of Bonn. The Plateaux of the Eifel and High Veen are, moreover, compressed and very rough, especially when these approach the deep crevices which ultimately lead into the larger valleys of the Moselle, and especially the Rhine, besides are studded everywhere with isolated peaks and entire and conically-shaped mountain ranges, befitting them very unfavorably for military operations upon a large scale.

As the system of the communication answers to the topography of the country, as just now sketched, it becomes evident that it is and would so be found the most widely spread in the valley of the Rhine, between Lauterburg and Mayence, and on the other side in the belt between the Rhine and the Maas. In the Eifel High Veen and in the Dog's Back it has fewer branches, while among the hilly lands, as well as in the Haardt, communications are mostly formed by defiles.

From the peculiar condition of the boundary line, as well as from the geographical relationship to adjacent objects, it is clear that military operations which are aimed at Paris by Germany, and at Berlin by France, can be undertaken by two routes: the one by way of the Bavarian palatinate of the Rhine, above Mayence, and the other by way of the Upper Maas in France *via* Luxemburg, in the vicinity of Duseldorff, or, *vice versa*. The valley of the Moselle, with the adjacent impassable portions of the Dog's Back and of the Eifel, confronts both directions of these military operations, separating both battle grounds from one another.

PART THE FOURTH.

THE PRUSSIAN AND FRENCH ARMY ORGANIZATIONS.

It is well known that France can throw an army upon the Rhine much easier than Prussia can, because the way from Paris to Saar Louis is but half as far as from Berlin to Saar Louis, and the yearly frequented camp of Chalons, as well as the strong and well mantled fortresses of Metz and Strasburg, (which since have capitulated) close upon the boundary of Germany, and facilitate essentially the initiative to such a mammothian enterprise. It was, therefore, on the part of the Germans, no useless apprehension of such surprise, as it would have forced them beyond the Rhine. But the haste with which the French diplomatists accelerated the breach of peace, upon which the declaration of war should immediately follow, a proof of their utter ignorance of affairs in Germany, especially of military organizations, prevented the execution of the attempt at a surprise which otherwise, beyond a doubt, would have become dangerous to Prussia.

France, however, unable to act as quickly as the voluble tongue of her diplomatists dictated, gave Germany time to rally her strength to a proportionate extent. The cause itself of their delay in action, from the declaration of war to the commencement of hostilities, was chiefly in placing the French army on a war footing, the consequence of an organization so extremely bad, that it frustrated the advantages that its greater strength in times of peace decidedly possesses over the Prussian. Single sections of the army, for instance, the guards, soon gathered their quotum of men from soldiers on furlough in and near Paris; likewise the Zouaves Turcos and the Foreign Legion, which sustain in times of peace their full strength; all these are quickly put in marching order. Even the infantry has, in proportion to the Prussian, far less reserves and furlough to gather.

Yet the draft requires a greater time, because the regiments have to draw their men, not from certain provinces close by, but from all over the country. In the Prussian military organization, however, each army corps is formed of men drawn from a certain province or county; for instance, Pomerania, Mark, Westphalia, etc., and the war material attached to it likewise from there. Such a system for the organization of army corps, divisions and brigades is unknown in France; their regiments receive their reserves as promiscuously gathered from all over the Empire. (Which, by the by, to California readers it may be interesting to remember, has two hundred thousand English square miles, with about thirty-six millions of population upon it, while our beloved State, Eureka, has one hundred and eighty-eight thousand square miles, and about one million thoroughly happy people upon it, who, by way of a past-time, always prefer bear-hunting to man-slaughter, and a serene happiness to the agony of ambition.)

Besides, in France there is no organization which reaches beyond the formation of a regiment. The tactical combination of army corps, the brigade division and corps connections, which in Prussia are permanent, have in the French army, at the commencement of a war, to be newly formed.

To these military defects may be added those of State. The Government is, in a manner, unnaturally centralized in Paris, which tends to suffocate and stifle all progress in towns and counties, by alienating the thousands of various officials there from their duty as free men, to be at all times personally responsible for their actions. Everything has to emanate from Paris, and unless it is there commanded, nothing whatever is done in the counties.

In Germany, especially in war times, every official throughout the Empire holds in readiness what could possibly, and on a sudden, be of him required by his immediate superior, so that as to the army, the fact may be illustrated to its full admiration, that although not a soldier of the entire army stood in the ranks on the 15th of July, yet on the 4th of August, the frontier of Germany, towards France, was found guarded in a manner that made a surprise on the part of the French an impossibility.

But France had been busy ever since Sadowa, to put her army, if not on a war footing, at least in readiness, and Minister Rouher never uttered a more truthful word than when he said that peace, at that date, existed only because Napoleon was not ready. May be he would have waited still further, if he had succeeded in gaining Prussia over to his plans in regard to the annexation of Belgium, and on the other hand, by so much waiting and inertness, could have been sure that the army would not have forsaken him. But the French army, ever since 1866, underwent reforms ; the nation had been roused from its security, although it was felt its present army system could not stand securely the shock of war, especially against Prussia. Said reforms were of a two-fold kind : either of a practical nature, like the introduction of the Chassepot rifle, the replenishing of the arsenals, the increase of stock of small arms, the change in the system of drilling, the rebuilding of eastern fortresses fit to stand the new inventions in cannon:—or again reached the basis of army regulations, the recruiting system, or amended the law to buy off allegiance to serve ; likewise the time of service in the army; the duty as reservist and the establishment of the Mobile or volunteer guard. All these changes were well conceived, but did not eradicate the evil. The permission to buy off service had been considerably curtailed, but the main defect in the French army system: the want of every kind of reserve remained unaltered to its former full and pernicious extent. As to the Guard Mobile, it was but a sorry imitation of the Prussian Landwehr system, which all military men have entirely condemned. Particularly bad had been the effect upon the military system of the expedition to Mexico, having cost so much money, and above all, having injured the French nation. The Government would not dare to state the figures it had amounted to. All that was done, instead of replenishing the lost material, large furloughs were granted to artillery and cavalry, which put the army into such a state that it required all the energy and indefatigable spirit of Marshal Niel, as Minister of War, to set things somewhat right. The Senate granted one hundred and fifty-eight million francs, and in 1868 sanctioned a loan of four hundred and eleven million francs. All this money had been expended on military purposes, as re-building of forts, manufacturing of Chassepot rifles and other war materials. To every regiment of the line were added two new companies ; a new regiment of Chasseurs had been formed so as to reach the former compliment of cavalry; the artillery augmented in 1867 by one hundred and twenty cannon, made in Austria and Germany, and a purchase made of thirty-six thousand horses, and in 1868 ten thousand horses and mules additionally. Marshal Niel then declared that but twenty-eight thousand horses more were needed to consider the entire army on a war footing. Probably that statement had been as incorrect as that there should be ready up to 1870 nine hundred and twenty-two thousand Chassepot rifles.

But there were other defects in the French army which were not changed by these amendments and augmentations of materials. Louis Napoleon had made his Marshals millionaires, and his soldiers pecuniarly independent. In 1855 he had introduced by law the horrid practice of a buying off service ; a miserable system, according to which every Frenchman could rid himself of military duty, by paying into the Dotation Fund the sum of two thousand three hundred to two thousand eight hundred francs, obliging the State to find a substitute for him. In order to do so, the State re-enlisted old soldiers about to quit, by paying them a bonus, increasing their pay, and then after the time of their additional service had altogether elapsed, granted them an annuity, so that army service afforded means, after a certain time, of making the individual pecuniarly independent.

The baneful consequences of this system to the French army, nobody more elaborately nor truthfully depicts and explains than Trochu, in his celebrated work regarding the French army. He shows therein that by it the consciousness of personal duty is entirely destroyed, when the State finds substitutes, and societies are formed which find such substitutes even for those who with little money can secure themselves against the fatal muster roll of conscription.

That the army had to deplore such comradeship taking the place of volunteers from all classes of society, is the natural consequence of such a system. Soldiers becoming grey in barracks cannot again become serviceable as industrious citizens of the nation, having alienated themselves from society, and not unfrequently become corrupted by vices emanating from idleness, especially bad whisky. Every ambition which might have been advantageous to both army and people is thereby wantonly destroyed and made naught.

The original intention of this system, which so signally has failed, had been to create an army personally devoted to the Napoleonic dynasty, needing no yearly additions and renovations, yet ruined the strength and the martial spirit of the army. Of the contingent of one hundred thousand men, which, since 1856, should yearly be got together, but twenty-three thousand appeared. Thus, the re-enlisted old soldiers footed up one hundred and twenty-five thousand men, and with other service added, viz., volunteers who choose the military career, officers, *gens d'arms*, foreign legions, in all about two hundred and forty thousand men. Then the military budget of three hundred million francs did not suffice for four hundred thousand men in times of peace, although, in fact, there were but three hundred and thirty to three hundred and fifty thousand in all; consequently, there was but room for one hundred thousand raw recruits, which was abundantly filled during seven years with twenty-three thousand men annually. In a military point of view, the natural consequence of this pernicious system proved to be the dying out of all strength of reserves. In times of war the army was without means to recuperate its strength from the people. Napoleon experienced it already during the Italian war, because in case of a war with Prussia at one and the same time, he had only sixty thousand men left, deducting the depots and fortresses, to guard the eastern frontier of France. Afterwards he tried his best to amend the fault. Why he did not succeed had two reasons—the one of a military, the other of a political nature. From a military stand-point it contradicted the custom of annually recruiting ninety thousand reserves necessary for a successful reorganization, requiring a devotion to the task of drilling on the part of officers and sub-officers, which is not at all part of the French character. In the other case, by drawing from and again returning to the nation, a full third of that figure would have given to the army the appearance of an army of the people, which did not at all suit the plans of Napoleon. He therefore adhered to the buying-off system with its old soldiers, and annually small additions, but endeavored to create a sort of army of reserve—this way, that by a decree of 1861, he divided the number of annual recruits into two halves; the one should serve a longer time and then be attached to the so-called active companies, while the other half should be drilled but two or three months annually, and later five months, and then with their flighty knowledge be dismissed, yet should stand ready in war times to serve as recruits. Thus Napoleon thought of having solved the grand problem of the organization of reserved bodies. General Trochu condemns it by saying it does not depend upon large ciphers, but upon the quality of troops. In 1869 the buying-off system was somewhat modified, and the old decree of 1832 reinstalled, which made it optional to the man on duty to find a substitute. The re-enlisting was abridged. After a five years' service the soldier should but serve another five years as substitute, and those which had entered a ten years' service should receive a situation in the civil service instead of pecuniary remuneration. Since 1865, the first demand would bring a contingent of sixty-three thousand men; the second, with five months' service, twelve thousand men. In this manner, and in obedience to the law of the first of February, 1868, which guaranteed after a five months' service a four yearly reserve, the army in nine years, therefore—1877—would have a strength of seven hundred and seventy-six thousand men.

But the duty to serve as reservist never suited French habits, while the Prussian soldier serves as reservist six years, and as militia six years. Marshal Niel then proposed to increase the Mobile Guard up to five hundred and fifty thousand men from all over France, consisting of infantry and artillery, two thousand men each company. They drilled, but could not be expected to stay more than a day from home. Their duty should be to represent and take the place of the army in large cities, fortresses, and on the coast and frontier, caring likewise for security within the country. It consisted of young Frenchmen, who did *not* serve in the army, together with volunteers, while officers and sub-officers were pensioned officers and sub-officers of the regular army there. Besides their pension they received a handsome pay for this particular service. Since the death of Marshal Niel this innovation is, however, neglected, as it did not receive the approbation of the people, especially in the south and west of France. General Trochu touches these defects as not only detrimental to the tactical advancement of the troops, but so personally. Styling the infantry the "Queen of Battles," he deplores their disregard. At first special annual recruits select their necessary arms, then the best drilled soldiers are attached to the guards, and finally each battalion of the line adds two special companies. The consequence is, that the four companies of the center form a feeble mass. Gen. Trochu succeeded in abolishing the latter so as to disperse them among the whole battalion as soldiers of the first class, but he failed in demanding for each battalion a company of efficient sharpshooters besides. Gen. Trochu explains the want of tactical education in French officers as follows:

"In our last wars our tactic was to allow the troops nobly inspired "to run for the battle-field; as soon as the first perished the battalion "advanced, but no longer compact, general dissolution ensued."

Incapable of flying, and likewise incapable of being cool and collected, they stormed onward to ascertain the cause of the effect. Disobeying the officers, they became commingled in large masses with the enemy, which paralized the action of their artillery and cavalry, upsetting the plan of the battle, and all the ramified and general combinations which their commanders-in-chief had made.

Gen. Trochu states that the cause is the nervous temperament of soldiers from bad habits acquired in Africa, reducing systematic military operations to a guerrilla warfare, and lastly as consequent upon the rigid rules of manœuvres in time of peace, perfectly useless in war.

While the French forgot the doctrine of Napoleon I, the Prussians studied it and added to its theory the experiences of the Crimean war, the Italian and the North American. The French adhering to the German idea or the old Dessauer, drilled continually in barracks, which proved to be of no use whatever in practice.

Although on the 16th of March, 1869, new orders were given as to the drilling of infantry, yet France knows of its rigor little more to-day than it did in 1792, which shows that France is by inclination less martially than peacefully and republicanly inclined.

PART THE FIFTH.

THE WAR IN DETAIL.

At the commencement of the war, the French army confronting the German, footed up about four hundred thousand men, although nominally, all reserves included, it was given at eight hundred and sixty thousand men. They comprised but eight corps in all:

Guards, under General Bourbaki.
1st Corps " Marshal McMahon.
2d " " General Frossard.
3d " " Marshal Bazaine.
4th " " General de l'Admirault.
5th " " General de Failly.
6th " " Marshal Canrobert.
7th " " General Felix Douay.

The North German army numbered four hundred and ninety-three thousand men, and one thousand two hundred and forty-eight pieces of artillery. The militia available at any time, two hundred and thirty thousand men. During war the body of reserves numbers one hundred and thirty thousand; in all, eight hundred and fifty-three thousand men. The South German army numbers—Bavaria, seventy thousand men, with one hundred and ninety-two pieces of artillery; Wurtemberg, twenty-three thousand six hundred men, and fifty-four pieces of artillery; Baden, twenty-one thousand six hundred men, and forty-two pieces of artillery.

The entire army, nine hundred and sixty-eight thousand two hundred men, with one thousand five hundred and thirty-six pieces of artillery.

Commander-in-Chief of the entire army is the King of Prussia.

1st Army Corps, commanded by General von Steinmetz.

2nd Army Corps, commanded by Prince Frederick Charles, of Prussia.

2nd Army Corps, commanded by the Crown Prince of Prussia.

4th Army Corps, commanded by the Crown Prince of Saxony.

First Army Corps of Reserves, commanded by the Grand Duke of Mecklenburg-Schwerin.

The Bavariam Army Corps, commanded by General von der Tann.

The Wurtemberg Army Corps, commanded by Lieutenant-General von Obernitz.

The Baden Army Corps, commanded by Lieutenant-General von Beyer.

SKIRMISHING.

> The watch of the Rhine gives the alarm;
> The great horn of Orlando is sounded.
> Let Alsace be mine, which does you no harm;
> With Metz and Lorraine the matter be rounded.—GERMANIA.

Small detachments of African Chasseurs of the French army crossing the German frontier on the 19th of July, were immediately driven back on French soil by German Lancers. The French, returning in larger bodies, skirmishing commenced near Saarbruecken on the 24th; at the village Gerweiler, south of the little river Saar, and to the west of Saarbruecken, on the 26th; and at Niederbronn, five German miles from the frontier, until the 30th of July, noon, when the first telegram was received from Trier, which stated that the enemy kept quiet. Later in the day, at five P.M., another telegram was received at Saarbruecken, which said that the German infantry had orders, in case of overwhelming masses, to quickly retire from Saarbruecken, the cavalry only keeping the enemy in sight. It was further mentioned that the French were concentrating to the east of Thionville, having vacated Gersweiler, after having been chased out of the forest of St. Arnual. Next day, at nine A.M., a telegram was received from Saar Louis, which informed the German commander that the French were beyond Forbach, with four regiments of infantry strong, one company sharpshooters, three squadrons cavalry, and one battery. The idea of the French had been to separate the Germans at Saar Louis from those at Trier, by destroying the railroad which runs parallel with the French frontier from Saarbruecken to Saar Louis and Trier, it being the only one which directly connects the latter cities. They attempted it from Forbach, a frontier town of French Lorraine, as it is situated opposite the Prussian frontier town of Saarbruecken, the railroad there being but two English miles distant from France. St. Arnual and Gersweiler, both Prussian villages, are situated between Forbach and Saarbruecken, while Louisenthal and Voelklingen are little railroad towns between Saarbruecken and Saar Louis. The Germans, of course, were equally industrious in destroying the French railroad between Saargemund and Hagenan, which traverses the Rheinthal (valley of the Rhine) down to the river Saar, and might have been very serviceable to the French in transporting provisions for their troops, besides possessing other tactical and strategical advantages.

Matters became rather trifling until the 2nd of August, when suddenly the French darkened the sun with the Chassepots of three divisions (about forty thousand men) and twenty-three pieces of artillery, under the heir apparent, with the tremendous intention of annihalating seven hundred and fifty solitary Prussian Leonidasians in the Thermopilan passes of that anything but gappy neighborhood. The fourth and fifth dispatches explain this affair earnestly: "On the "second of August, ten A.M., the small detachment at Saarbruecken "was attacked by three divisions and the town bombarded with "twenty-three pieces of artillery. At noon the heights, and at two "P.M. the town were duly deserted, the detachment retiring to the "nearest station. Loss comparatively trifling. At the same time it "was mentioned that Emperor Napoleon had arrived at eleven o'clock "before Saarbruecken."

On the same day the King of Prussia had arrived at Mayence. The command over the three army corps, duly entrusted by him to General von Moltke, subdivided, as they were, into the first, the northern, mostly centered in the county of Trier, resting on the fortress Coblenz, and commanded by General von Steinmetz; the second, the central, centered in the Bavarian palatinate, and resting on the fortress of Mayence, and commanded by Prince Frederick Charles; and the third, the southern, centered in the palatinate, and resting on the fortress of Rastatt, commanded by the Crown Prince of Prussia; the venerable Moltke took command.

THE BATTLES.

Having issued his orders to the three army corps to advance upon the enemy, the southern wing, under the Crown Prince of Prussia, began, on the 4th of August, to close on the enemy at Weissenburg, Alsace, and storming the adjacent strongly fortified Gaisberg, defeated the French division under Douay, in a very decisive manner. Continuing to advance, the same commander, but a few days later, on the 6th, engaged the French in the first great battle, the memorable one of Woerth, in which the third army put to flight the first corps of the French, under Marshal McMahon, while on the same day the Northern army, under Steinmetz, with death-defying impetuosity, stormed the heights of Spicheren, defeating Frossard, in command of the second corps of the French. The natural consequence of these thorough victories had been that the entire French army was forced to retreat towards the river Moselle.

To counteract the terrible blow which French official statements of victories, instead of defeats, had dealt to the dynasty of Napoleon, the

Emperor decided upon transferring the command of the French army to Marshal Bazaine.

Be it remembered that the genius of Moltke having so placed the German army as to form with its three army corps a wide half-circle, of which the center under Prince Charles had not as yet been in action at all, Moltke now commanded the united forces to at once close upon Metz, the virgin fortress of Germany, taken from her three hundred and nineteen years ago, and one of the principal strongholds of France.

Although the French army had entrenched itself near the river Nied, on French territory, it, nevertheless, vacated the neighborhood, crossing the river Moselle, near Metz, upon the cavalry of the Germans arriving before Metz, Pont-a-Mousson, and Nancy, together with sections of the army from Strasburg. Here it was, before Metz, where in three days the redoubtable Germans dashed to pieces the old glory of French arms, and transferred upon themselves the grim visage of Mars, who, wherever he thrones, holds the crimes which are heirs to barbarism in subjugation. On the fourteenth of August, General Steinmetz threw into confusion three French divisions, at Pange and Courcelles, forcing them back upon Metz. On the sixteenth, Prince Frederick Charles having crossed the Moselle but a day previously, annihilated in twelve hours, at Mars la Tour and Vionville, the martial pride of selected French troops, while on the eighteenth of August the venerable hero, King William, in grand command of the whole slaughtering force, attacked the French in their fortified position to the west of Metz, and wrung from them in nine hours time the victories at Gravelotte and Razonville, beyond a doubt for ever fatal to the French nation as a ruling war power in Europe.

From that hour history asserts it that the French had to yield the continental power of Europe to Germany as practically consequent upon this very victory, and owing to the decided superiority in the leadership over the German armies in comparison with the one over the French. Leaf after leaf was duly plucked by Germany from gory battle fields in victories without end, in self-defence of her national independence, and to wind the wreath of laurels which shall forever grace the broad forehead of Germania, as the future continental safeguard of peace, enlightenment, and constant exercise in humane deeds of love. The newly-born sister of America will, in due time, receive the baptismal of political liberty, without restraint, as the natural consequence of the prodigious effect of universal free schools, to be realized in times of peace only; but until then, in the face of the awful fact of being closely surrounded by less advanced, and consequently murderous and warlike nations, on the continent of Europe,

Germany has to stand for possibly a generation to come in the unenviable position of a gaoler.

It has, furthermore, to enforce law and order at home, to prevent a disturbance of the prolific soil against immature republicanism, best denominated "the unripe fruit of knowledge instead of communism." The sound seed is long ago sown; like upon a bed of flowers, the young plants in due time appear and become visible in masses upon a sudden, so shall Germany produce in due time a compact mass of principally equally informed millions of men, who, in their real, consequently social amiability, shall so have universally advanced, and so be considered sufferable to each other, while coming in contact with one another in public life, as to be able to neutralize the chilly fog of the spirit of caste, which hangs over all aristocratic atmosphere, and obscures the happiness of all on the sole account of that uneven distribution of knowlege. Dispersed, the genial warmth of the ever charitable sun of enlightenment, will quickly mature reason so as to make the obvious truth fully bloom in all its pristine loveliness, that every man living at any time upon earth shall not merely be his own independent sovereign, but respect the sovereignty of every other man he sees living next to him, near him, far and wide.

When on the evening of the last named great day, the Pomeranians, the bravest of the brave, on a par in physical strength with our stalwart backwoods-men, stormed, under the very eyes of Moltke, all the heights to make sure of victory, when the legions under Bazaine waved for shelter towards the walls of Metz, (Moselle) when at last the greatest warrior of the age, the aforesaid Moltke, testified to the historically astounding truth of a complete victory: Suddenly appearing before the King, merely saying, while he deliberately wiped his forehead with his handkerchief, "Sire, the battle is won, the enemy retires,"—then it was that the French war power was crushed, and European civilization rescued from the fangs of surplus crime and that mediæval superstition so easily practiced in blood.

Germany, the world may rest assured, shall never have to blush before it, as having had other intentions than to prepare Europe for self-government, but not until that distracted division of the globe is thoroughly competent for the task through education and general enlightenment, which shall, like with us, ensure a peaceful permanency to the republic of nations, shall she relinquish the grasp upon the sword to awe the vast millions of Europe in obedience into law and order, nor cease to prevent unmerciful masses from blaspheming beforehand with carnage, and revenge the sacred republic and her worthy disciples in France and everywhere else in Europe.

Bazaine, with a greater portion of the French army thrown into

Metz, McMahon, with the remainder of the army thoroughly prevented from joining Bazaine, the Germans found free the road to Paris.

Prince Frederick Charles immediately tightening the ring around Metz, the 3d army corps, under the Crown Prince of Prussia, began at once to march upon Paris in a south-westerly direction, in company with the newly formed 4th army corps commanded by the Crown Prince of Saxony, moving northwardly along the river Maas.

Suddenly their movements had to be changed, as McMahon having received reinforcements, had quitted the Camp at Chalons (Marne); but instead of hastening to cover Paris, he endeavored to again reach the north, intentionally of joining Bazaine. However, the Crown Prince of Saxony barricaded his way on the 27th of August, near Busancy, which afforded the army under the Crown Prince of Prussia the necessary time for returning from the feint, and joining the former, enabling the Germans to conjointly finish the army of McMahon at Beaumont, and in a manner that a junction with Bazaine was henceforth not only made impossible, but the single road into Belgium at all left for the disorganized columns of the French to possibly effect their escape upon.

Bazaine likewise had not been idle. On the 31st of August he debouched with all his forces, left at his disposal, in an easterly direction towards Servigny and Noisseville, trying with all his might to break the iron fetters of the Germans. However, the heroic resistance of the division of Kummer, and of the East Prussians under Manteuffel, impenetrable like bristling cactus hedges, forced him after a fight of thirty-two hours duration, to return to his prison. During the night, from the 31st of August to the 1st of September, the Prussians, Saxons, and Bavarians, forming upon the banks of the river Maas, encircled the French army in a wide space to the east of the fortress Sedan (Maas). With the dawn of day, the terrific battle, of which history shall forever make mention, commenced with what was designed to either capture or route the entire French army and finish the war. The French driven from the villages Floing and Bazeilles, before a fire out of 800 pieces of artillery, the circle of the German army became smaller and smaller, until the enemy within, inclusive of Napoleon, was hurled like Caffres into a kraal, in hurried flight into Sedan. Forsaken by his own soldiers, who had lost their irresistible *elan*, and under circumstances had become demoralized, Napoleon wrote to the King of Prussia expressing himself willing to deliver up his sword and himself as prisoner of war. *Maximum imperium sibi imperare.* The capitulation of the army followed next day; Marshal McMahon, being dangerously wounded, General

Wimpffen delivered up the army, 83,000 men, with 4,000 officers. A few hours later Napoleon appeared before the King of Prussia.

The Napoleonic empire broken upon the battle-field on the 2d September, 1870, which news Palikao kept secret for forty-eight hours, ceased to be on the 4th of September a national institution of France. With it disappeared the Empress, her son, Benedetti, Ollivier, and especially, Grammont, and as usually the republic was declared.

In the most brilliant manner have victories upon victories justified the Prussian military organization of 1860 as the greatest providential fortune which ever Germany was favored by. It has served as the mightiest aid towards the accomplishment of the union of Germany. The few croakers against it in Southern Germany have disappeared as if by magic, and are not any longer noticing the bard Count F. Filippi de Faby, who resides at a short distance from Berlin, in No. 22 Place Napoleon Cherbourg, who tried to chant a poem to them:

> D'un Napoleon, la gloire
> Vous voit encore abatus:
> C'est toujour la votre histoire
> La seul de vos vertus.
> Vous pensier d'etre invincibles
> Soit dompté peuple trop vain!
> Pour toi, restant inflexibles
> Nous gardous les bords du Rhine.
>
> [Exit Napoleon and his bard forever.]

Created in 1860 and improved upon and introduced into all Germany in 1866, the Prussian military organization has saved Germany. Through it the country was enabled to appear upon the frontier with an overwhelming army, to surprise and defeat the single divisions of the enemy in constant succession. The enormous number of reservists and militia put Germany in a position to immediately fill voids which a murderous fire had made, and without allowing a weakening of the army of operations to take place, made it possible that strong divisions of reserve could enter France, and large numbers of companies of militia could occupy the long lines of operations and repossess those portions of territory which had lately been occupied.

The North German divisions of militia alone amount to over 200,000 men, and the South German divisions over 30,000 men. That they are all very competent has become known even abroad, especially so they have proved at the siege as well as in the close battles before Metz. Germany would have had no chance of success in a war like this, in which it not only depended upon victory after victory to prevent the enemy from recuperating, but to hold the ground which had been conquered, which comprised pretty nearly one-third of France, if it had not been for the Prussian organization of the army. It has not only created an army of unsurpassed numerical vastness, but every soldier was fit to be called one, which alone culminated in the success of subduing the French upon their own ground.

PART THE SIXTH.

THE FRENCH REPUBLIC.

It appears reasonably certain that no monarch can fill the vacant chair of Favre! Had Favre at once remained as President of the republic instead of Thiers—a former Minister of Louis Phillip—being substituted, not only would the rebellion from the 18th of March to the 19th of May, 1871, not have occurred, but the republic would have been maintained quite satisfactorily to the majority of the people. If the republic cannot command respect by virtue of the law, how can a future monarch protect the law without access to force? It is therefore reasonable that the republic be maintained and thus peace made lawful, without a name as President, whose antecedents were monarchical, and who as such must be obnoxious to the very people who with glad consent declared and voted the republic on the 4th of September. Besides, to return to monarchs themselves whom the French nation indulged in only for vainglory of their arms, is now made impossible since the Napoleons, so to say, self-made monarchs by success of arms, and not of blue blood, are likewise legitimately and consistently obliterated from their memory. The second Napoleon in rule having filled the right scale to an overflow of misery for the nation, justice now lifts high the left scale of the first Napoleon, with his martial and especially his political successes, as based and consequent upon his ambition and meddlesome diplomacy, which succeeded so long in alienating the Southern German States from the natural tie of the Northern, upon the obtuse plea that the humanization of mankind, heterogeneous as to nationalities, could be effected *without preparatory* education—under monarchical rule—in other words, by rude force.

As to Germany, the world will admit that in regard to the Union of Germany, it is not the offspring of fear of Prussia on the part of the Southern German States, but is the natural consequence of enlightenment having attained its principal height in Prussia, diffused itself through the North as well as through Bavaria, Baden and Wurtemberg, and is daily encouraged in by the example of America, where about eight millions of citizens reside who are of German origin.

(As to manifestations of rejoicings of the latter at the Union so cemented by brotherly love, they were indeed touching in the extreme.

The torch-light processions in beautiful San Francisco—a distance from Germany of just about half around the globe—were large enough, on several occasions, to suffice to illuminate the hearts of all Germany as now seen from the Cathedral of Strasburg, and make them confident as sympathy can only.)

Again, the conduct of the revolutionists in Paris, proves conclusively that the greatest freedom from caste cannot aid the Republic at all, unless the people become universally enlightened, and consequently peaceable, by means of a radical reform in school education, and make it everywhere a municipal law that the poorest of the poor children of the million have free and unpaid access, to it. The pedigree of civilization rests upon merit, as merit upon knowledge, and knowledge upon developed reason through education in peaceful times. It will place itself where it belongs in progress, aided by the Odd-Fellowship of the appreciation of the worth of man, in this enlightened age, which knows naught but of merit. That merit has but one towering ambition: to please God !*

---

* Diverge to the very antipodes of the globe, and, for instance, place God's child of a Cannibal of the Solomon group off Northeastern Australia, whose parent, to-day, habitually partakes of man food, into civilized hands at a very tender age, give it education, and nourish its divine soul with love, and it will be in proper time as useful a member of society as anybody else. But should an uncharitable aristocrat by heart, although republican by name—an ignorant anthropologist, who, vexed at being unable to find out whether Adam and Eve, names which shall signify the first pair of the human race, who lived and were created to live the short space of time upon earth, had been brown, yellow, red, black or white, where, and especially when those two had been living, if such an ante-mundane visionary should get hold of the little one, then, of course, it is not to be wondered at, should he be all his lifetime afraid of the anthropophagic propensities of an innocent child's late royal savage great grandfathers.

Forgetting that the Mongolians settled in Europe though comparatively to the Jura period but a few years ago, he is incensed at the Chinese in China remaining again concealed, and won't even associate with him there, nor of their own accord visit him here, until he shall have proved to them in their own vernacular, which is necessary for him to do, in order to introduce an effect upon their understanding, how much better he is than they are, and in what his superiority over them exists, and more than that, shall have convinced them of it within the top of their cues. How wonderfully he will do in China, where they pretend to have never heard of earthquakes in Java, or the Red Sea flooding the globe, the dense millions then of Eastern Asia not having been communicative, and with whom a few days, synonymous of a few thousand years later, Vasco de Gama and Magellan found that virtues existed which it must have taken ages to acquire—for instance, that hunger is with them interpreted by cheerful labor, a good appetite by health ; thirst is assuaged by tea, and quarrels by smoke, and love, the priceless treasure of the heart, is not a ware which is vended in Sultanic callousness, and who as one nation foot up a concourse

History now continues its pages of this war, as unwisely waged by the Republic of France. It is, therefore, the second period of the war. Before it so does, reference to important events which have occurred in the east of France, take due precedent. Just as little as it had been possible for the French armies to resist upon the open battle-field the efficient precision of the German artillery, could the fortresses in the north-east of France do it, which it was necessary for the Germans to take. A number of them had capitulated up to

---

of 400,000,000 people, possessing a literature without an alphabet, and a language without a grammar, thus realizing the solution of the greatest enigma ever heard of. As to countless centuries, during which the Government has been in the hands of State philosophers, and the vernacular dialects have been abandoned to the laboring classes, how he will be startled to find that the Chinese language is, notwithstanding, by no means the most intricate, cumbrous, and unwieldy vehicle of thought, that ever in spite of eighteen distinct dialects, obtained credence among other people including himself.

The fact is, it is for this Government to enlighten the remainder of the civilized world upon the immediate consequences so multitudinously resulting from steam, now permanently connecting the great race of mankind in Asia, inclusive of Japanese, and exclusive of Hindoos, (as being the latter taken care of by the British) nearly 450,000,000 of people, with all the chances of an appreciation of our system of civilization, from which consequences the realization of our hopes of success of progress among mankind at large may be safely predicted, upon one condition, viz., *that the Chinese language be introduced all over the less populated civilized world.* It being the language spoken by a living people numbering 400,000,000, would be far more useful in the end to know than any language except the English ; and as to Latin and Greek, the wisdom derived through them from those defunct pagan nations might be found, upon close study, considerably exceeded and excelled, for what we are really aware of this day, by the Chinese classics, and at once much valuable time saved to the LIVING AGE. A people so very ancient and great in numbers, who carry with them, wherever they happen to go for a minute or two, three standard virtues of our civilization—Peacefulness, Industry, and Sobriety—should not be reasoned with by the sword by any nation, as stamping the civilized and reasoning world in their eyes as far more uncivilized and unreasonable, than they themselves are, at least surely were, previous to this century, in that particular respect, and fully explains that, for the present, the Chinese are not a migrating people, and when they do, proudly enshroud themselves in their ancient habits, not finding the civilized world at all comprehensibly superior to themselves.

Another reason is this, that they, when traveling, acquire knowledge of the English language, and interpret falsely our civilization after their own concretely, prejudiced fashion, because a mere smattering of a foreign language, sufficient in daily life, is quite insufficient to draw wisdom from literature, nor adequate to do justice to and appreciate the virtues of a people, while we, altogether, tapping in darkest ignorance of the Chinese language, presumptively judge at random from hearsay, knowing in reality next to nothing ourselves personally of them. All this accounts that the Chinese contribute nothing to our civilization, except eatables and wearables, nor voluntarily and gladly allow the civilized world to benefit them, because of ignorance of their language, and prejudices of every sort against them, as consequent upon general ignorance of their literature. That China and Japan are redeemable

September, 1870, after a resistance of more or less duration of time—but two of them, Strasburg and Metz, had not. Being strongly fortified, they fell into German hands much later, and not until after a long and laborious siege. Already in August the Government over the two provinces of Alsace and the German part of Lorraine, had been duly and justly transferred to Germany, as one of the necessities and consequences of the war. Not only are the people of Alsace and Lorraine originally German, whom the sacred duty to the Union require that they should be annexed, no matter how long a time they had been alienated from her, but, by abridging them from France and adding them to Germany, the numerical strength of the former became duly diminished, while that of the latter augmented

in time to republicanism, through adoption of our civilization, appears very encouragingly certain from the virtues aforenamed, which they very universally possess to an astonishing degree, and the friendliness which their Governments and peoples show America in preference to Europe, which they view as a torn-to-pieces conglomeration of small nations, very far inferior to them in compactness, and as they conclude, *from constant wars*, in all other respects. No! our honor now forbids to rest, since steam affords us a constant opportunity of coming in close contact with them, until we can explain to them in their own vernacular why we are the civilized people, of whom they would and should profit, morally, socially, and materially, and thus gain upon them the adoption of our American principles of civilization, and the steady customship of innumerable articles of commerce, especially the consumption of our impenetrable forests, which, on the Knitchpack, in Alaska alone, would pay for the little outlay of $7,250,000 ten-fold to begin with, and which, otherwise, would stay there until the next flood.

The antipathy which the civilized world has against them to-day, as absorbing labor to the pecuniary detriment of our people, would last forever, as consequent upon the impossibility of nationally and familiarly associating with them as yet, on account of the prevailing ignorance of their language, and our pardonable prejudices against their tastes, their habits, and their manners, in consequence of having, so to say, but now come in earnest contact with them since the creation of the world, which reciprocated antipathy befogs the true interests and enlightened duties of two halves of mankind.

The time has come for the ice of clannishness and intolerance—the offspring of ignorance—to melt, before the genial warmth of an ever-progressing, universal enlightenment, and the question forever and ever truthfully answered. Has God created two halves of mankind, that they should live estranged upon this earth?—that they should live in enmity, or be the laughing stock of each other? Has the aristocrat ever charitably conceived it that the savage lives by the same grace of the Almighty Creator of the illimitable Universe as he does? And that, consequently, he should go there and befriend him, and consider the Samaritan promptings of such an act in the light of a performance of a filial duty to God, and himself as a gentleman. Besides, what would our civilization really amount to if we could not make more money out of barbarians than they of us? On the other hand, in what does Europe benefit America? Setting aside the immigrant question, in what would it so do, suppose we had no commerce with Asia, with Oceanica, and with Africa? Perhaps the aristocrat will condescend to answer candidly! Again, how those

to approach to and form an equal balance of power of strength among the two nations, which, for the sake of peace hereafter, was, more than any other reclamation, absolutely necessary, and, therefore, demanded of France to comply with.

The hue and cry which arose against this proceeding among civilized nations, had a treble origin, all of which three reasonings were not alone unjust, but wrong altogether.

Firstly. The republicans all over the world thought it their duty to be with the Republic of France, as Napoleon had left with no possibility of a return; who, having once not only abjured the Republic,

---

Chinese and Japanese yearn to *learn* of us, the Japanese have lately best shown. Therefore, it is our turn, indeed, to quickly learn, if not Japanese, at least Chinese, as being a vernacular spoken by a ten times larger nation than the Japanese language is diffused among, teach it in all public schools of America and Europe. Waste no more time upon dead languages than is materially considered absolutely necessary. Our Oriental students coming here to study Webster, Clay, and Sumner, and finding us bending over Plato, Cicero, or Demosthenes, would politely substitute the great Chinese Confucius, and with all the etiquette of a devout Salaam, leave for home by the next mail steamer.

The smaller scholars in our schools would be far more amused to learn Chinese than any European language, for the reason that the writing is so contrived as to denote by the same character the sounds of each of the nineteen different words, all of which it equally represents, and is, therefore, very easily acquired. It is likewise known that it is of no great use among the multitude in China who cannot read, which would be of so much greater advantage to our people in the end.

At present it appears that of all the great scholars of the Chinese language, outside that mysterious fraternity, there is probably not one who to-day can converse in six of those aforesaid eighteen dialects, or could either orthographically write or interpret an important State paper without the assistance of a teacher. Alas! Those teachers, who are they? So far to foreigners in China, on account of prejudice and mistrustfulness on the part of the Chinese, for reasons above stated, the teachers which can be obtained are obviously but the very scum and refuse of the Chinese literary body, the plucked of the examinations, and the runagates from justice or tyranny. These are engaged at a lower salary by foreigners than they would obtain among the Chinese as Secretaries to a high official, if they were otherwise suitable; and if they are calygraphists, or speak a tolerable idiom, or pronounce with a certain purity of accent, (although they have to be unavoidably feared as domestic spies, repeating all they see and hear) they are blandly respected by some confiding Sinologue, who maintains them because he can't help himself. If one of those Chinese philologists should happen also to be the son of some small mandarin, he becomes to his pupil a very great authority on Chinese politics. Chinese politics! Good! Non-intercourse! which signifies that all mankind is barbarous save themselves, because they can do without the outside world of 600,000,000, and have so done for ages, together with the Japanese, while we cannot do without them, because we need their teas. The above teacher is, at the same time, a Petronius of Chinese ceremonial. Papers are indited, and foreign policy is shaped according to the response of this oracle. The Sinologue who derives his inspiration from this source, is again taken as an absolute authority by the civilized world in general. He has, furthermore, to think it his official duty to adopt, while he is in the flowery land, what he is given to

had ever since availed himself of his sovereign power to gratify dynastical pride at the expense of the prodigal trust of a confiding nation. That from under imperial robes, thus folded a republican heart, should designedly have disguised itself, harboring the noble intention of setting Europe free after France should have conquered its heterogeneous millions and annexed them to France, upon the example of America absorbing into the folds of outstretched brotherly arms the emigrant from any portion of the terrestrial globe, the world has long ago eschewed as a base imposition upon its credulity, and therefore execrated the Napoleons.

The idea of monarchs and conquerors taking America as an example! Why, America, no more than a Free Mason or an Odd

---

understand are Chinese customs, and to amuse himself the best way he can by pitying instead of studying the Chinese anti-flooded, rather antique and interesting ceremonial of 400,000,000 peaceable, sober, and industrious people.

Returning to the moral principle of republicanism as resting upon enlightenment, it is considered the first, highest, and strongest pillar of truth, which reason builds through all ages, that, the human race has equal rights and duties. An universally educated country will always guarantee an easy going republic. As to France, it has less idolatrous spirit of caste, and consequently is more self-possessed of a manly appreciation of the principles of republicanism, than any other nation in Europe. Her people are proverbial for graceful, social manners, and a jovial, hilarious spirit. Proofs are, her various attempts at a republic, while every where else in Europe, ignorance, and strange to say including France—among 280,000,000 of people—and their want of all personal influence and power, in consequence, was hithertofore so pitifully discernible that it could not much more than be thought of by them, far less be attempted with the remotest hope of success. Republicanism is altogether the personification of gentility. It is universal *par excellence*. The definition of that word is Freedom, is Christianity, is Masonry, is Odd Fellowship, etc.; in short, is everything reasonable, good, enlightened, amiable and independent. In the United States of America every born American is a gentleman by the breath of liberty. The formal European finds it out in about a score of years; the poor, however, feel it upon landing that the Americans are not the only ones so born. In the meantime the aristocrat suffers dreadfully from *ennui*. Everybody labors but he: the effeminated or prejudiced European does not; at least not with that natural ease with which the born American performs that wisely ordained intellectual duty by which he guards himself against sin, until the habits of the European are entirely changed by the ever-tossing wheel of time. Then only has he benefited by his travels, and then only does he stay where he is and is genteel. As labor, demanded by the physical condition of man, is a wise peremptory necessity, so it is destined to serve as the promoting power of virtue and morality, being the whetstone of the intellect, when obeyed in cheerfully and voluntarily, mentally or manually performed. It consequently creates that gentility which is but a double progress—an augmentation of the attributes of civilization and an increase of the comfort and happiness to the individual being.

The application of time constantly devoted to either mental or manual labor, leaving no room for a waste of energy from idleness and its degrading effects of slothful habits leads to the attainment of wealth. That there are among the 40,000,000 Americans already more substantially wealthy individuals than can be

Fellow, thinks of forcing people into the union of brotherly love! It might as well ask a grown up Apache, or a bigamist, or a criminal, or an habitual drunkard, or an infidel, or any other vicious or crazy element, to be their brother! No! If charity demands pity of man and nations in the sight of God, it likewise demands prudence not to expose a good cause to the infallible ruin from seduction by what is barbarous and fatal to it. Charity strives, by all manner and means, to civilize and befriend man wherever he lives forlorn, in order that he may appreciate freedom for his own and for the good of mankind.

---

found among 280,000,000 Europeans, is traceable only to that fact of an universal love of voluntary individual labor, which is instigated by personal independence in a free and fabulously rich country. Such men always appreciate freedom, enjoy wealth, and live peaceably. Every gentleman is peaceable when he is at work. It includes a fearful courage at the same time, when he is disturbed at it. Attack a peaceable man, a peaceable nation, and the aggressor is either cut by the frown of independence and the etiquette of disgust; or, if murderously inclined, suffers extermination forthwith. So it was in the war for the defense of the Union in America, and so it is now for the defense of the Union of Germany. Deplorable as the cases are in this enlightened age, yet they admit of no alternative. Revenge is unknown, unforgiving heart's revenge. A civilized man governs himself, and never offends. The law is made for ungovernable men. Every gentleman lives within the boundary of decorum, therefore within the pale of law and decency. In the United States of America law is subordinate to the immense masses of gentlemen, who do not need it except as a guarantee for the comforts of life to be officially testified to. As to a fear of the law, it is not so understood in America at all. A gentleman fears nothing, averring rightly that fear is the consciousness of guilt—the remembrance of a bad action; a gentleman is never guilty of anything which might be called bad; he communes with God and governs himself before he acts, which leads to lawful and civilized actions—makes friends instead of enemies wherever he lives, which is sense well applied, and which education, good company, especially Ladies', and an appreciation of art, science, and the beauties of nature, develop in him.

PART THE SEVENTH.

WHY PEACE WAS NOT CONCLUDED AT SEDAN.

The republicans, in other words, the entire unbiased civilized world, became at last convinced that the republic of France had better yield the two provinces to Germany, because these were, as already stated, of German origin, had been German property once summarily taken, had now in monarchical fashion been legitimately re-conquered, and by their population diminishing France and enlarging Germany, adjusted the physical strength of both nations upon a satisfactory equality absolutely necessary for the sake of future peace in Europe. They argued correctly that the republican cause had lost nothing by the cession, if considered that Germany to-day like Great Britain stands upon intellectual and moral grounds, disguisedly nearer the principles of a legitimate, lawful, law-abiding and therefore permanent republic, flourishing in peace only, than France visibly does in spite of the latter, remaining ahead of both Germany, Great Britain with her colonies, as well as the entire remainder of nations upon the continent of Europe, with the only exception of Switzerland and Montenegro, because it is one to-day, and the others are not, which guarantees to a republic wherever it is in reality established, the sympathy of the civilized world with the United States of America at their head, acknowledging its legitimacy.

Viewed from this consistent point of view, the idleness of the SECOND ARGUMENT against the acquisition of Alsace and a portion of Lorraine is likewise exonorated and explained as follows: The two provinces conquered from Germany posterior to the foundation, in due historical rotation, of the French monarchical power over the continent of Europe, as founded by Henry IV, within that period of his reign which dates from 1598 to 1610, and was possible only and consequent upon the decline of Spain at the time of the government of Lerma, and which French traditional power has been perpetuated as such through the three consecutive dynasties of the Bourbons, the Orleans and Napoleons, up to the 4th of September, 1870, when it was duly ceded to Imperial Germany by the force of this war—as to these two provinces republican France now says, it will not spare an inch of territory. What does it mean? Do they think the people of Alsace and Lorraine are consigned to perdition?—are irredeemably lost to republicanism? which principle embraces not only Germany, but mankind!! No. It means nothing less than that the Republic will continue in the footsteps of the principles of monarchy, power! and is not sure of its permanency, being harrassed by monarchical claimants and their troublesome adherents. Anyhow, it is very inconsistent and very unwise if considered that Germany never yet proved an aggressive spirit, nor that any monarchy ever yet dared to attack a legitimate republic, and in this case, Germany, a disguised republic as to comparative intelligence and fitness, and as such peaceably inclined towards all foreign nations, except those which shall withhold German non-republican elements from immediate cession to the fatherland, gives as great a guarantee to Alsace and Lorraine for the future happiness of the prosperity of their population as France does.

Monarchical Germany can wage war against those foreign nations only which call a Germanic population their own, as Austria, Russia, Holland, excluding Switzerland only, where the Germans are already living under a republican form of government, and need no preliminary fostering and care, and which aforesaid nations shall refuse that liberal pay or exchange for their Germanic elements, which Germany is duty bound to prodigally offer for the sake of the fulfillment of her sacred duty to complete the union by gathering together her Germanic elements, but never will the Emperors of Germany wage war upon civilized nations with an anti-feudal aggressive design upon territory, and indulge in a Cæsarian lust for barbarous conquests generally.

When thereupon the French republic argues: "You do not take the German Swiss from the republic of Switzerland, why do you take the German French from the republic of France?" The answer is, that if France to-day had Alsace and Lorraine, it would to-morrow forsake a third time the glorious republic and be monarchical *toute suite*, and as such would be unjustly unforgiving, war inclined as before, try as quickly as possible to recuperate, endeavor to form alliances with all Europe if possible, and march like locusts by millions in balloons, with the white flag or the lily flowers pending, as the case may be, to Berlin as if nothing at all had lately happened. That explains it for the very good of the republic, why Emperor William did not already conclude peace at Sedan, because he could not get from the Republic of France those strategical points and lands necessary for the defence of Germany in case of a third overthrow of the republic. He had history as well as knowledge of the character of the monarchically inclined portion of the French people to guide him, and although he proved by the acknowledgment of the republic, that politically he had confidence in its permanency, yet he had duties to perform towards Germany which were peremptory in the face of the Bourbons and the Orleans being visibly about. He is by no means unamiable on that account, or at all a conqueror in a barbarous sense; if he was a second Barbarossa he would have conquered the whole of France at once, and kept it, instead of which, he was satisfied with the symbolical act of a centaurian gallop around the Arc of Triumph, like a man of principle and not of retaliation, in memory of his father, Frederick William III, and the entire Germany, balancing accounts with the shade of the first Napoleon, and then quietly retired without further noticing the captive one at Wilhelmshœhe.

When, therefore, the Germans marched on from Sedan to Paris, and there around the Arc of Triumph, to finish the conquest over the former general monarchial power of France, still smouldering in a warlike and revengeful republic, the sturdy architect of Germany did, simultaneously of time, a signal service, and a great deal of good to the republican cause, which it is obvious he must have had at heart, when he acknowledged the young republic born under his very eyes, weighing correctly the chance of her permanency against those of a disgraceful collapse as dearly affecting the peaceful growth of future Germany. It demonstrated confidence in the majority of the French nation, while it pointed to the olive branch of peace, which, above all, should be the greatest adornment upon the forehead of the Goddess of Liberty that they Republicans should not further resist as unworthy of their principles.

Has ever a brave nation, or really a brave man, a good cause, a noble intention, been disgraced by defeat? Can, for instance, a republic like America ever be disgraced? By whom or by what? One should like to know. Has Christ not forgiven the very people whom he could not with his two hands prevent killing him? So should every republican be as good as Christ, and every man be a republican, until there is not a hand lifted to strike, which makes self-defense of the other unnecessary. That is why the civilized world are called Christians, that we should follow his example ; that, in case of helpless misery in life, of defeat, or even of death, among barbarians, we possess that inner courage—fortitude, resignation, and faith—which is ready in a good conscience at all times to cling in the exquisitiveness of a loving caress to God, the Creator of the Universe, by whose inscrutable wisdom we at all here do live and die. Does man ever forget, or is so blind that he can't see, that he is God's son, as well as anybody that is and was created by His Grace? That each tiny plant, each worm, lives by the same inscrutable grace only, for purposes which are mysterious and yet are not? That we live now while others lived in the remotest past? What arrogates to man superiority over the brute creation? Man's equally distributed possession of the divinity of an originally healthful reason, endowed with for the purpose of living happily himself, and to make others happy, while so living upon earth. Therefore, to act unreasonably, is to be cruel and bad, non-republican and warlike; and no civilized being likes to thus stand degraded within himself before the great Creator.

The world now acquiesces in the cession of those provinces, as the population of Alsace and Lorraine is not lost to republicanism, no more than we do consider the entire civilized world lost to it; on the contrary, it is steadily preparing for it as all mankind is plainly and reasonably redeemable to it.

That by an augmentation of Germany the cause of republicanism in Europe should be retarded, because Germany is as yet monarchial, is not dialectical, therefore unlogical and altogether wrong. The enmity of the cause of republicanism in Europe has disappeared, with the disclosure of the Germans acknowledging the Republic of France at the very moment of complete victory, generally so seductive an opportunity for crowned heads to forget their vows, except in this glorious case of Emperor William. History has duly marked it that from now dynastical rules are no longer considered stringently necessary. It really and incontestably proves that Europe is far advanced in civilization; it is constitutional; therefore on the high road to republicanism. It is, so to say, a political syllabus got rid of; it is Protestant freedom, politically and nationally practically applied. It is in accordance with liberalism, as far as the untutored millions are daily more quickly becoming reduced in numbers to digest it, and be thankful for it to God only. With the King of Prussia transmuting into an Emperor of Germany, and acknowledging the French Republic when he had it in his power to absorb the whole French country, all political hierarchy and infallibility to rule by especial divine right is left with the empty chrysalis. That act speaks volumes of rational hope for Germany itself; it is a just tribute paid to the fact of the existence of enlightenment, and a constant increase of liberty in Germany; it is the unmistakable dawn of freedom. Thus reason wings itself etherially high, throwing off all dogmatical restraint which hinder its flight within the realm of bliss, and lives not to conquer and to die, but to live and to love. With such a version of the condition of Germany and all Protestant monarchial countries, the THIRD ARGUMENT against the acquisition of Alsace and Lorraine is already principally refuted, which advanced the theory that the Roman Catholic religion would be assailed, as if religion was a terrestrial body, which could at all be slain. Roman Catholics have found out by this time that Protestantism and Liberalism go there hand in hand at the same rate as Roman Catholicism and Liberalism go hand in hand in Italy. In the same proportion that beyond a constitutional monarchy a nation advances into the highest order of civilization, the fitness for self-government, which are the republics all over the civilized world, so does religion advance to prepare the mind of civilized man to a direct pious communion with God. In republics it is precisely where Roman Catholics and Protestants hinder each other, if at all, then very harmlessly indeed, and certainly not politically, of any consequence. Their occasional hatred in this age is simply nonsensical, because it is not any more the offspring of ignorance and bigotry, but an old, decrepid habit which is fast becoming exploded and extinct. It is on a par with the hereditarily diffused blue blood of aristocracy, which fears an inoculation from the lowly, forgetting that it is their crime of not having educated the masses, which criminal neglect created hithertofore all the insecurity, hatred, and general disobedience to law and order. Besides, Protestants and Roman Catholics have more to do than to hate each other, when they reflect a little that far over half of mankind await their eloquent persuasion.

Inasmuch as republicanism testifies to civilization and signifies it, so does Christianity strive to make proselytes among the nearly treble number of heathens in Asia, Africa, and Oceanica, where Roman Catholics and Protestants pioneer hand in hand with this noble cosmopolitan purpose in view, of redeeming them to our faith. There is no heart so obdurate which would not cease to hate when minutely reflecting upon the vulgarity of such antipathy and animosity among Christian brethren, that it involuntarily reminds one of a poem by Tiedge, about a hundred years old, which always elates and edifies wherever and whenever it is read:

PIETY.

Alas! should'st from Thy grave
   Thou greatest sufferer! arise;
Once more teaching, bent upon a stave,
   A wanderer through life, so wise!
Should'st Thou behold the mischief all!!
   How they pervert the truth, this gift
Of wisdom, plain, yet so beautiful,
   Flowed from your lips, the soul to lift!
How they disdain all love's affection,
   Press persecution from Thy teachings,
Which teach to love and bless upon reflection!
   How they forget all tolerant doings,
Which bear with faults, love what is good—
   And Thou, alas! dejected by contumely
Up to thy very last in Cypress blood
   Hast exercised upon Thy murderers truly.

> Thou would'st now shed a tear
>   So bitter!—as ever from Thy mortal eyes
> Then fell upon the olive mount so dear.
>   And should'st Thou here your teachings
> Yourself reveal—they would: these elves
>   And pseudo exegetics hearken to proceedings,
> Who hear no one but themsèlves—
>   Should'st Thou, however, dare to differ;
> Not do, as bid by their presumption,
>   Not believe in Thee, except through their transfer—
> They would surely crucify you twice.

Free schools to all liberally paid for by a government, acknowledged as the divine right of mankind to their heavenly dowry, "reason," which education enables them to further develop in active life for the purpose of being able to lead a happy and useful existence, and to cosmopolitanly appreciate republican life, as guaranteeing the independence of man while it rests upon the individual ability of piously revering the commands of God so obvious to that effect—is the first doctrine of civilization practically applied.

The French nation hithertofore barricading the way of Germany to uniting her elements, had to be disabled by physical force of continuing it in the face of the degree of civilization attained to in the 19th century of the Christian era. The French had to be thoroughly disabled for that purpose; it was absolutely necessary, and one may as well assert, the will of heaven that the provocation to this war, which accomplished the union, should have been given by France. Now while the iron is hot, the Austrian Germans, the Russian Germans, and Holland ought at once to return to their original national allegiance; the quicker it is now enforced by Germany, the better, for France recuperated, unless she remains republican, might ally with Austria and Russia for the same vainglorious purpose of conquest as of yore. But if fourteen millions of Austrian Germans, together with all the other non-republican German elements outside of Germany, as that country to-day shows its configuration of forty millions, are added to it, then peace is permanently established in all Europe, and with the rise of another generation the Germanic race in Europe may be predicted shall be republican. In the meantime Germany and England unite to allow education to take a deep root, and whatever revolutionary disturbances may take place in Europe, they will rightly pronounce them premature, and take care of the north of Europe. United Italy, on the other hand, will take care of the south of Europe, being now unmolested by France—a republic—so that Spain and Portugal, together with the rest of the south of Europe, may not be disturbed in their earnest strides for progress. Republican France is equivalent to peace. Every republic is equivalent to it.

On the other hand, nobody will dispute in Germany and England that the love of country is sacred; but to say, to prefer a monarchical government to a republican, and to try to prove it, that life and property, law and order, are safer and greater, would show an effeminacy of manhood, which is quite unnatural to any sensible being, and has but one parallel—that of a rich bachelor, or amiable maiden Lady to make the world believe they live happier in their single blessedness than if they were married, as if they knew anything at all about it. Again, take a widower or widow Lady deprived of his or her playmate by death or lawful divorce, and observe how quickly they again embrace matrimony at all hazards. So it is exactly with an intelligent and moral man who once has lived in a republic, and should change his domicil and again live in a monarchical country; how he yearns until he has returned to the republic. As to the United States of America, there is not a man who ever lived in sunny California is absent abroad upon some occasion or other, who would not readily exchange the world for his lovely Eureka.

One of the most potent reasons why the remainder of the civilized world acquiesced in the cession of Alsace and Lorraine to Germany, was besides the impossibility of preventing it by force, the justice of the case itself, which clearly demanded it. The idea to deprive a victor of his booty, after the entire Germany had been exposed to the chances of ruin, and had to offer upon the altar of Liberty a life, a human life, of greater value than the universe, and more than that, tens of thousands of such sacred lives, ignorant people only could have harbored, or worse than ignorance of theirs that Germany, which had just now positively proved a sagacity and strength greater than any continental nation in Europe possesses, could so have been reckless and soft as to leave a conquered country empty-handed, and all out of womanish mercy and sickly sentimentality, knowing, as all the world does, that thereby it would have actually encouraged France to a repetition of the same sort of intent to at an early convenience invade Germany as in 1870. Better ask a tiger to give you back the lamb; war is barbarous and conducts itself as such, *vice versa*.

This gandering arose at Sedan, and continued at Paris (beautiful Paris, a third of which demolished by exasperated French citizens) that Germany could afford to be magnanimous and abstain from humiliating France. Of course she could, but see France five years hence, as hinted before, resume the same business of frightening peaceable nations. No! the Bowie-knives had to be kept; leave France to-day as strong as Germany, and there is *never* any peace. For that reason Germany now adds all her Germanic elements, domineered over by foreigners, for the purpose of being not only equal but stronger than France, in order to arrive at a permanent European peace. It is then immaterial, in a strictly political point of view, whether France remains true to the present republic or not.

As Germany does not aggress for purposes of conquest, surely France cannot be parceled out like helpless Poland. So Germany took pay in those two provinces, and Metz as the key to the European powder magazine of wars, for no other reason than duty to the German fatherland.

This action, was, therefore, never intended to humiliate France, no more than the First Napoleon ever intended humiliating Germany by overrunning the whole country. It is by no means retaliation, which is as unchristianly as war itself, but simply proves that war lurks in ambush, and that the Christian disciple is insincere.*

Germany acts, therefore, extremely wise, if she continues to absorb all Germanic elements throughout Europe, for the one purpose, and as swiftly as possible: to outnumber France in population, as France might forsake the Republic, for the third time, and again go to war.

---

* Rather should man ensnare the strong lion and rhinoceros and other felines and pachyderms living upon earth, although even those cannot be exterminated because they are there and eminently dangerous—no more than the most destructive arms can exterminate war, despotism and revenge; the guillotine aristocrats, or a Bartholomew's night, the Protestants. The weapon successfully wielded against fury, injustice and intolerance is equal knowledge. It is by reason that man and nations shall govern himself and themselves, and overcome difficulties as God points to the aforesaid physically thousand-fold stronger creation that it shall be so.

Look upon the street, and you will find the divine nationality of the race—the promiscuous multitude of human beings of equally puny height within an inch or two, as being equally destined by God to live socially, contentedly and hopefully in the world. It is the clue to the truth that the rights of man are the same which knowledge—the developed reason—explains and duly expounds. You will find them following each other through this life like monkeys crossing a stream, to continue upon the other side in safety and harmony. That swarth for man is wisdom —to live peaceably everywhere and enjoy life socially. It is reason fully developed. It is the Eden found upon earth; the lee-side of the storm of war and individual passion. *It—is—wisdom—how—to—live.*

As God gives life, he takes it—and nobody else dare.

PART THE EIGHTH.

THE CAPITULATION OF STRASBURG AND METZ.—NAVAL ENGAGEMENTS.

The province of Alsace and the German portion of Lorraine were therefore added to Germany, and Strasburg and Metz taken, as peremptorily necessary for future safety. The fortress of Strasburg, so bravely defended by its commander, General Uhrich, from the 11th of August, yielded the keys on the 28th of September, at last. Neither the investment nor a dreadful bombardment, which unfortunately devastated a large portion of the city, with its columns and treasures of arts, proved of avail to induce the heroic General Uhrich to surrender. A regular assault had to be made before success crowned the heroic efforts of the great German General von Werder. Hoisting the white flag to the world renowned Strasburg Cathedral, at the immense height of 430 feet, it being the 27th of September, 1870, reminded Germany of how, 198 years ago, that celebrated city was torn from the German empire by France. The day of that anniversary, the 27th Sept., 1870, the fortress mournfully capitulated. A month later the energy and perseverance of the German troops were likewise and equally brilliantly recompensed by the success before Metz. After having nine long weeks invested the place, apparently an invulnerable one, suffering hunger and cold, and exposed as a target to a deadly fire of grape, and having repelled those energetic assaults of Bazaine's, which he ventured on even after the battles of Noisseville, of Peltre, of Mercy, of St. Remy, and at last of Woippy, on the 7th of October, which latter lasted nine hours; then it was at that critical moment that the misery of the besieged becoming an ally of the Germans, induced the proud Marshal, with 173,000 men, to capitulate. At the castle Frescaty, on the 27th October, 1870, this event received its historical signature, and the second French army corps, like the first one, was sent into captivity to Germany. So the laurels faded which Bazaine, the victor of San Puebla, had not long since usurped in Mexico, while Prince Frederick Charles had patriotically gathered new ones at Metz, in France, similarly to the Crown Prince of Prussia, the victor of Orleans, had gathered his, both receiving the rank of Field-Marshal Generals, as memento mori in due consequence of their services to the German nation, and the well deserved sincere thanks besides.

Less prominent than were the successes on *terra firma*, yet not without importance to Germany, were those at sea, in the memorable summer and fall of 1870. General Vogel von Falckenstein, having been appointed Governor-General of all the lands upon the German coast, issued, on the 24th of July, a demand for volunteers to join the marine. Then torpedoes were laid and the coast properly fortified to prevent the possible landing of the enemy, and the little German fleet lay ready at Kiel and Wilhelmshaven to cope, to the best of its ability, with the by far stronger one of the French, relying somewhat upon the ignorance of the French of the geography of the coasts of the North sea and the Baltic. Strange to say, the French fleet was really unsuccessful. Barely two engagements deserve mention : the one off the island Ruegen, and the other off Weichselmuende, the harbor of Danzig upon the Vistula. In the West Indes, off the Moro of Havana, the German gun-boat "Meteor" preserved the honor of the German flag in a bout with the "Bouvet." The German ships "Grille," and "Nymphe," had done similar brave acts in the German waters.

In the meantime, the second period of the siege of Paris had commenced to develop itself against the Republic of France.

On the 19th of September, the larger portion of the German armies had reached Paris in forced marches, forming a huge and strong girdle of some forty odd English miles in extent around the city, which the statesman under Louis Phillippe, the venerable Thiers, had once metamorphosed into one of the strongest fortresses upon the globe. It was about that time that peace appeared near at hand, for suddenly the President of the French Republic, Monsieur Jules Favre, appeared at the German headquarters, soliciting an interview with Count Bismarck respecting the chances for an armistice. But their auspices were not good, and the non-republican conduct of the French at the time, of not yielding what was demanded by common sense and equity, and had and should be granted to the Germans as victors, frustrated their accomplishment. This political blunder on the part of the young republic has already been explained at large upon previous pages. Suffice here once more to say that the world at large approved the cession of territory for the purpose of the equalization of the military strength of the two nations, and a payment of five milliards of francs for damages besides, for what, in fact, cannot be at all refunded: the divine lives of human beings, having died by thousands, contrary to civilization. Therefore, war continued, and more sanguinary in proportion to the resistance offered than before. In fact, all France arose and followed Gambetta, to try what was neither wisdom nor republicanism, but savored much of hatred and revenge instead of patriotism. Besides, as might have been foreseen, it proved unavailing.

The damage done by the French to France in these national efforts, in the way of destruction of roads and property, was a severe lesson to the young republic for having disgraced the sacred republican doctrine of peace, having parliamentary ways at her disposal to force Thiers to leave. The excuse for self-defense on their part was inadmissible, because the Germans had been found ready to accept peace against being paid for what was fair, and besides were known as not harboring any intention whatever of an opprobrious kind, as touching the independence of France. As to the frantic fury of the French, in trying to prevent the organized German armies of continuing their besieging operations before Paris, it was, as might have been expected, ineffectual.

PART THE NINTH.

THE SIEGE OF PARIS, AND THE BATTLES AGAINST THE ARMY OF THE LOIRE.

General Trochu having been appointed Commander-in-Chief of the besieged forces within the walls of Paris, by the Republican Governments at Paris and at Tours, had an army of at least 350,000 men under his command, inclusive of National and Guards Mobile. The numerous and good artillery within the forts consisted mostly of marines. Scarcely had the Germans completed their investment, when the sorties of the French commenced, demanding incessant attention on the part of the Germans. The latter, however, soon made their work in a manner thorough, that, after destruction of the subterranean telegraph lines, the French had no other way of communicating from Paris with outside France than by balloon, which was rather an out-of-the-way mode of communicating, on account of accidents from shots of the enemy, and also under circumstances of being so very uncertain. After the King of Prussia had moved his headquarters to Versailles, the residence of Louis XIV, the sorties of the French became often—ostensibly to exercise the troops, but intentionally to break through the enemy's lines. On the 7th October they pressed towards Malmaison; on the 13th towards St. Cloud, which latter castle was destroyed by their own grape from Mount Valerien, and on the 15th towards Villejuif. The battle on the 21st October, near Malmaison, in the presence of King William, was very severe, as were those near Le Bourget, on the 28th and 30th October, which place had to be stormed by the Prussian Guards in the most heroic manner, signifying severe losses of the latter in officers and men.

The month of November went off comparatively quiet, because the newly-formed provincial armies had to receive their first teachings from the mythological Mars; the forts, however, keeping up a lively but expensive cannonade, which resulted in a dead German costing France about 80,000 francs.

Gambetta had gone early in October, by balloon, to Tours, to there organize three new armies, known as the army of the Loire. The venerable Garibaldi, the celebrated General of Italy, appeared among them, and, with his two sons, took command. But the defense, nevertheless, degenerated into a guerilla warfare, in spite of the remonstrances of Garibaldi, through the formation of bands of Franc-Tireurs, or sharpshooters, who, lying in ambush, like at Ablis and Chatillon, tried hard to decimate the gallant Prussians, by murdering them. It was, therefore, luck, indeed, for the Germans that Metz fell into their hands the latter part of October, which enabled them to send a great army against them to silence them forthwith. Part of the entire army of the Germans remained before Paris, the other under Prince Frederick Charles and the Grand Duke of Mecklenburg, was directed to operate against the army of the Loire. Thus, the battles of the Germans against the French Republic were fought by three armies stationed: the first, easterly, south of Alsace, the second along the River Loire, and the third in the North of France.

After Strasburg had capitulated, General von Werder had the command assigned to him over the Eastern army, consisting of Baden troops and Prussians, with whom he cleared Alsace the first half of October, in the skirmishes at Champenai, Nompatelize, Epinal, and other places, leaving nothing of weight but the strong fortress in the mountains named Belfort, the siege of which was commenced later on the 8th of November. Upon this, General von Werder, reinforced by the reserve army of General Lowenfeld, advanced south upon the Eastern army, under General Cambriels, and upon the Garibaldians. The first he vanquished in the fight at Oignon Lake, and the latter he drove out of Gray, invested Dijon, (Burgundy) Montbeliard, and Dole, and then spread his operations toward the west, the upper part of the River Seine. On the 22d November, the General was attacked by the Garibaldians, at Nuits, who felt somewhat more confident since their surprise at Chatillon. He stood it bravely, so that when a few days later the venerable hero, Garibaldi, repeated the attack, near Pasques, trying to circumgo his location near Dijon, he, the commander of Strasburg memory, scattered the Garibaldians on the 26th and 27th November.

Now succeed the battles in the south, the great battle-field of this war, which occurred from October 1870 to January 1871. These were indeed the most difficult, complicated and laborious of the whole campaign. Already in September raids of cavalry had been made against the army of the Loire down towards Orleans. In the early part of October the Bavarian General von der Tann, reinforced by the Crown Prince of Prussia, marching their respective armies south and engaging the enemy in victorious battles at Toury, Etampes and Artenay, forced the latter to retreat towards Orleans. That city they stormed on the 12th of October, after an engagement of nine hours, which sent the French across the Loire. Shortly afterwards, north of Orleans, General von Wittich annihilated a French army at Chateaudun, and taking the city, invested Chartres on the 21st of October. Towards the end of that month the German armies in the south, especially those under Prince Charles, had been largely increased after Toul, Soissons and Metz had been taken, and the end of the war supposed to be near at hand. Such was, however, not the case. The energy of Gambetta must have been of an enormity truly admirable, although it was not wisely conceived, for not only did he manage to largely increase the army of the north, under Bourbaki, the army of the west under Keratry, and the army of the Loire under Aurelles de Paladine, but he put the same on a regular war footing. The latter General, who had already early in November more than 80,000 men under his command, tried now to cut off the Bavarians at Orleans, he having a vastly superior force at his disposal, and if successful, to reach Paris forthwith; circumstances favored him so far that General von der Tann had to give up Orleans, and after the fight at Coulmieres had to retire upon Toury, although the Grand Duke of Mecklenburg had put to flight part of the army under Keratry, on the 17th of November, near Dreux, and General von Wittich had forced back a second portion of the enemy's army upon Chateauneuf. Matters stood thus doubtful, when Prince Frederick Charles came to the rescue, and thoroughly routing Paladine on the 28th of November at Beaune la Rolande, while on his way to Paris, prevented a serious conflict, for General Trochu, informed of the intention of Paladine, made those energetic sorties at Brie and Champigny on the 30th of November, and 2d of December, respectively, in consequence of which history has taken note that these have been unfortunately very sanguinary, but nevertheless were repulsed. Simultaneously with these events General Manteuffel cut off the north army under Bourbaki, preventing it from reaching Paris, by defeating it at Amiens.

In spite of all these disasters the French were by no means discomfited. Dismissing Aurelles de Paladine, and gathering the disheveled masses, (which Prince Charles in the meantime had promptly pursued, retaking Orleans on the 4th of December) under General Chanzy, in the west, and under Bourbaki in the east, it had been shrewdly decided to intrust the army of the north to the most intelligent general of France, General Faidherbe, as ceded to him by General Bourbaki. The French army was now divided into two commands, instead of as formerly into three. General Chanzy endeavored to stay the advance of Prince Charles upon Tours, which city, the Government fancying defeat possible, had wisely quitted in time, and adjourned to Bordeaux, but was defeated a second time in battles lasting four days--from the 7th to the 10th of December—at Beaugency and Marchenoir, retiring towards le Mans (Orleannais). The iron Prince, together with the Grand Duke of Mecklenburg, continuing their pursuit, chased the French out of Vendome on the 15th of December, and took possession of the whole line from le Mans to Tours. Not, however until January, after many skirmishes had taken place, was the army of the west thoroughly beaten. The battle of le Mans (province Orleannais) lasting four days, finished Chanzy and the army of the west. The severity of the winter had assisted the Germans as it did of yore the Russians against the first Napoleon, besides the Germans are, as were then the Russians, used to such horrid cold weather—France, therefore, could not be saved in that direction. As to the second chance: the army of the north under Faidherbe had to succumb to the superior vigor of the Generals Manteuffel and von Goeben, although the former, General Manteuffel, had had to evacuate St. Quentin (Picardie) after having invested Rouen, the great manufacturing town upon the River Seine, famous for its iron works, and Dieppe, a small seaport. Yet he managed to throw the army of the north, fully 60,000 strong, upon Arras, after the French had suffered a second defeat near Amiens (Picardie) on the 23d of December, two days before Christmas.

General Faidherbe, nothing daunted, tried it once more, early in January, to attack General Manteuffel, but the Germans stood the brunt well near Bapaume, on the 2d and 3d January, 1871. General Manteuffel, upon being transferred to a command in the East, General Goeben took charge of the German army of the North. He, likewise, was attacked by Faidherbe off Cambray, but the Germans repulsed him a third time in a battle near St. Quentin, (prov. Picardie) which lasted seven hours, and this time in a manner which was equivalent to a rout.

While all this took place, Paris having now been invested over three months, yet unwilling to give up the keys of the city, having managed to get at sufficient food some way or another, and being determined to resist to the last, approached its fall. From the 19th to the 22d December, General Trochu debouched, but without success. The German artillery at last did the work effectively; it destroyed the strong position of the French upon Mount Avron on the 27th and and 28th December, and on New Years day 200 cannon sent the molten gifts of Vulcan into Paris and the forts, with compliments from General v. Kameke and the Prince of Hohenlohe. Paris was paralyzed. Once more, on the 19th January, the French tried it near Mount Valerien, but were again defeated under the very eyes of Emperor William of Germany. General Trochu had now to leave his command, and President Favre appeared, on the 24th January, at the headquarters of the Germans at Versailles, to negotiate for a surrender. Paris then had been in a state of mutiny. At midnight of 27th January firing ceased. Next day the armistice was agreed to, to last three weeks, which handed Paris over to the Germans after a siege of four weeks. From said armistice, however, the Eastern battlefield was excluded.

A constitutional assembly was formed at Bordeaux, which should at once decide upon the future form of Government, in order to be enabled to make peace.

The 18th January, 1871, had its especial significance. The King of Prussia had been, on the 16th December, 1870, unanimously declared Emperor of Germany by the German Reichstag, after a proposal by the King of Bavaria, on the 9th December, 1870, to all the German Princes and free cities of Germany. On the 18th January the victorious Emperor celebrated the historical event in Versailles, only seventy years after the Kingdom of Prussia had at all been founded.

The month of January was likewise decisive in the East. There stood Garibaldi with his volunteers, reinforced by the new army of Lyons, under command of General Bourbaki, whom Gambetta wished to throw back the weaker numerical strength of Werder, should retake Belfort, (Alsace) and march into Northern Germany. Good ! the idea was by no means bad, for danger there was ; therefore the Germans quickly sent aid to Werder, by the 2d and 7th army corps, as he had to retire before overwhelming forces from Dijon upon Vesoul, in order to cover Belfort. But even before all these auxiliary troops were upon the spot, the heroic Werder had repulsed Bourbaki, in a three days' fight at Montbeliard, which forced him to retire to Besançon.

The second plan of the French to unite with Garibaldi was likewise frustrated. The brave General was attacked at Dijon by the 61st Regiment, and had to remain there, which enabled the 2d army corps to arrive unobserved, and place itself between the two combatting armies, and in a manner that, with Werder, surrounded the entire French army under Bourbaki. There was then no other alternative left for the latter but to either surrender or retire into Switzerland. On the 1st February, at Sombacourt and Frasne, Bourbaki fought desperately and lastly, but he was thoroughly defeated, and his demoralized army had to disarm before the Swiss General Herzog.

The celebrated, and very bravely defended fortress of Belfort, in Alsace, capitulated, on the 16th February, with free egress of its brave garrison.

The eight months are gone—the war finished ! What horrors ! and yet how small the hope that it has been the last. May the Omnipotent console those loving mothers, sisters, wives, and brides. Man cannot, nothing on earth can ; not a deluge of tears could. May he send to us all a genius, who shall know how to prevent bloodshed among civilized nations !—since everybody reads the Bible, and nobody follows the doctrine of peace.

When it is asserted that in 180 days 156 fights, and 17 more or less battles occurred, that 26 fortresses more or less strong were stormed, 373,000 prisoners made, 6,700 pieces of artillery taken, and 120 standards and other military emblems were conquered; that these astounding victories gave back to Germany what is hers, Alsace and the German part of Lorraine, together with Metz, and reimbursed the nation for the costs of the war with about 1,300,000,000 thalers, equivalent to five millards of francs, and enlarged Germany to 9,900 square German miles (a German mile is about equal to $4\frac{1}{4}$ English miles), with a population of 40,000,000 upon it, and divided into twenty-five States, then it may be rightly supposed that the peace made at Frankfort-on-the-Main is based upon the physical impossibility of France of ever again attempting to disturb it.

Setting aside the moral improbability of the republic of France, so far forgetting her advance in civilization as to again fall back into the fetters of monarchical rule, it is a national and sacred duty incumbent upon Germany, to propose without delay to Austria and Russia the cession of the German provinces upon the most liberal terms, at the same time peremptorily insisting upon compliance with such a natural and patriotic demand. It is supposed that nearly twenty millions of population of German origin are living under foreign monarchical rule. There can be no peace until these have returned to their national allegiance; besides, an alliance might be arranged at any future time between recuperated France (should it not remain republican) Russia and Austria, as it is so easy to tear to pieces what blood upon battlefields has cemented, and monarchs dispute anew. As monarchy signifies war, and the republic peace, and the one is based upon physical and the other upon moral strength, so does it appear as extremely unlikely that peace can be applied to Europe as long as Germany is not among monarchical nations the highest power of physical strength. Bound as she is then to metamorphose herself into a correctly acting republic, she is, at least, up to that time a bulwark of force and a tower of strength against Austria, Russia and France, should the latter prove a sham and undue the republic. As this last hypothesis is now unlikely, as France takes a high rank as a republic, having succeeded in quieting the rebellion, Germany will easily manage with Austria, Russia, etc., either peaceably or by war.

But their Germans must belong to the general nation at all hazards, and upon any condition. It is the great desideratum of the age, the centralization of the nationalities. It is done in the interest of civilized mankind; it will accelerate age by age the promulgation of the commands of God, who created neither nations nor countries, but the independent being upon the one land of the earth. France, at present impotent, and as a republic, unwilling—Great Britain the natural ally of Germany in case of war with Russia, Austria and the remainder of European nations—war will not be resorted to on that account, and the Germans be released against any amount of money and non-Germanic territory.

As to Poland, she has a more natural future among the broad Sclavonic race which it is the destiny of Austria to henceforth gather; and as to Russia, she has a similar one from among the more dispersed and heterogeneous nationalities of the entire northern Asia.*

The world wishes France well; it is fully aware of her misfortune; it has ascertained abroad what her grief is at home. The *Nouvelliste* in Rouen, repeating the words of the novelist, Alexander Dumas, who acquainted the world with the grief of France in the following touching passage, says: "For the moment it's clear, that the invasion has conquered and muddled us, that the rebels have cleaned us out and dishonored us, that the country has lost two of its most beautiful provinces, that the most elegant third of Paris is in ruins, that the capital of the civilized world has proved again in 1871 what it did in 1793, viz., that it stands always at the disposal of horror, and that our people possess the same qualifications as Kings do, viz., to learn nothing from misfortune. Public disasters, private misery, irreparable losses of life, of inspiration, of love, of hope, of luck, of labor, of faith, an enormous foreign debt, a senseless one at home, humiliation, disheartedness, doubt, apprehension, gloom, high and low, and everywhere gloom, dispersion of families, dissolution of parties, a rout of principles, and especially a double current ; of an instinctively

---

* The world has a right to exchange opinions in regard to the future of nations, which have undergone a radical change either in prosperity or adversity. It is especially inclined to wish well to the unfortunate as in accordance with the towering principles of civilization. It is one of its most ennobling traits to be charitable. As in individuals, so in nations, to sympathize with the afflicted and to be always ready to stretch out the helping hand to the needy without waiting to be called upon so to do, shows the true disciple of Christ, applies practically the finger sign of heaven, so feelingly illustrated by the act of the Samaritan, as the sweetest nutriment to the living soul upon earth. The greater the delicacy with which these heavenly inspirations lead to the act of charity, the more the donor prevents the blood mantling upon the cheeks of the helpless recipient—the more delightful is the moment of ineffable bliss of having done one's duty in a grandly religious manner, and the more visibly does Providence reward him upon the spot. As it is at the same time the equally distributed chance to all of heavenly wealth, it proves that the principle of benevolence is the developing element of gentility and general civilization, planted by education, and germinated by religion.

double need of reprisals and rest ; of retaliation and resignation, of hatred and love ; that is, in a few words, our situation at this hour." And, possibly, it is ; but France is not lost no more than a gentleman is. A mind full of faith, repentance, energy, and health, lives ; it views crucification as purification ; it draws strength from defeat, and fortitude from sorrow ; it is the sunlit-smiling earth after the raven blackness of a tempestuous night ; it is, above all, a momentarily clearer conception of the hope of an eternally blissful hereafter, as powerfully convinced of by the inimitable existence of life, of the moment in so grand and obviously perishable a world in common with us, awaiting the further will of Heaven, to continue altogether, and thus realize the purpose of creation.

France is a republic, and Dumas is too severe when he says she has learned nothing from misfortune; she has learned a great deal: she has learned to conquer the rebels, what she didn't know when she allowed Napoleon III to forsake the republic scarcely twenty years ago, which proves that there are to-day far more enlightened men in France than ignorant ones. In whatever country that is the case, freedom is permanently at hand. Educate! educate! continue to educate every child living, and pay for it by law, and you will strengthen the republic and uproot vice upon this earth, circumgo the intoxicated profligate gambling parent (the cause in all countries of the growth of vice in children), crime and wars ! Education and peace live upon reason and love; their strength cements the union and the universe, and social life becomes not only bearable, in a rigorous conventional point of view, but shows its divine nature ; as men approach each other naturally, the All-wise wills it that there should be no distinction except the sweet rivalry of how to add to the usefulness and happiness of one another, until the moment of life, which is in God's hand, is by Him recalled. France has leveled these distinctions, by force upon Napoleon, disowning his vows to the republic, and be permitted so to do, instead of like Washington standing by the side of the people and be forever beloved. Great Britain, Germany and Italy will level them peaceably. France—the Gallic race—is impetuous; the Teutons are not; they await all the effects of universal education upon the worth of man to appreciate freedom quietly and resignedly. Their govermental heads at least mean well or else the world had to despair of their sincerity ; they change the diet of the patient in proportion to his convalescence. They await the arising of the million in the terrestrial garden of free air and liberty with joy and hope, as every physician does who is not a charlatan, and can premise the time of convalescence as far as study goes, and the Almighty's heavenly will in the case commences.

Although France is a republic, and as such synonymous of peace, and has proved her inner strength by the subjugation of her improperly educated brethren, yet she may as well remember for a while longer the significant words of Picard in his proclamation of the 27th of February, announcing the entry of the German troops into Paris. The confused monarchical spirit among some incorrigible minds, is still a heavy incubus upon an easy-going young republic, setting aside the customary dynastically selfish attempts of the three dynasties plotting an entry, to either one of which it would be idle to suppose for a moment that the French nation would forget itself so far as to listen. Picard said, "We conclude peace with the expectation of "future retaliation," at least many so said with more or less distinctiveness, and many French who do not say it think so beyond doubt. It would be difficult to teach those who pushed the war, living upon glory and brooding over the chances of enlarging the territory of the country, to henceforth think otherwise. This great knowledge of the character of many, guided Bismarck in asking proper security for peace in the shape of territory belonging to the republicans. To continue the war to the knife was as unwise of the republic as it was impolitic and useless. Has ever a sensible man doubted the bravery of a Frenchman? Of what use was, then, an idle attempt to struggle with the giant of fate? All it did it showed lack of wisdom. To cope with impossibilities, is to compare man, frail as he is, struggling in the grasp of a pachyderm. If the French made peace upon this comparison, and not for wisdom's sake, then they are really to be pitied, for there are three realities, which are as clear as daylight, that they cannot regain—what they have once lost—as Germany is too intelligent to idle and vegetate upon war laurels. It is ahead of France now, and will labor to so continue.

PART THE TENTH.

THE CONSEQUENCES OF THE WAR UPON FUTURE CIVILIZATION.

Above all this war has demonstrated to France the complete military superiority of Germany. France possesses really better small arms; but the great physical strength of the soldier, the more thorough organization of the army, and the better discipline and the superiority in moral qualities, has everywhere been acknowledged has given victory to the Germans. Those are, indeed, superiorities which cannot be easily acquired, even in a long time, especially if the national character and public affairs are not exactly favorable to the performance of exploded war measures; viz., upon universal military service France is not likely to decide, on account of its principles of republicanism.

France has no inclination for this earnest exercise of military duty. A preponderance of physical strength is, therefore, put out of reach. The French people diminish slightly in physical strength, as this war has evidently shown. Increase of population advances much slower in France, in percentage, than it does in Germany. The exhaustion in France of disposable men took place quicker during this war than it could be possible among the Germans, setting aside that the French enlisted old men and small youth promiscuously. Besides, in a few years from now, after the Prussian system of the organization of the army shall have been adopted by all Germany, both North and South, Germany shall have far more numerous armies than at present. The times are not yet such as to disband soldiers and make working men out of them. The Rhine is not quite so broad as the Atlantic! This alone will make the French think twice before they overthrow the republic and commence a dynastical war.

The second reality is the changed boundary and the new constitution of Germany. The boundaries of Germany hithertofore, as good as if they stood widely open, together with the political separation of the South from the North, were a great seduction for France under either of the three dynasties to wage war with her German neighbors. To-day Germany has finely locked boundaries, and stands united to a man against the combined continent of Europe.

What must be her security of peace to Europe when the foreign non-republican Germans are added to the Union ! Then she may force Europe to disarm, and be the first to do it.

The third reality is the financial impossibility. In the French Budget for 1870, the interest of the national debt absorbed already twenty-four per cent. of the entire income ; army and navy, twenty-eight per cent. At present, the costs of the war, so it was stated at Bordeaux, footed up three and a half millards of francs, besides the five millards which she has to pay to Germany. At five per cent. this enormous debt of eight and a half millards of francs adds to itself annually 425,000,000 of francs. The ease with which she lately paid the first installment of the debt to Germany, although it proves proportionately large wealth, and but little impaired credit, yet is the damage done by the rebels fearfully great, nor was the destruction of property, both private and public, by any means small, which the French in their eagerness to defend Paris, rashly considered necessary to destroy, in order to keep off the enemy. Likewise the lost material of war, during the campaign, upon both battle-fields, as well as in the fortresses, has been of note. As all this will be felt for many years to come, France cannot retaliate even if she was not republican ; she has, therefore, to *reduce* the expenses of the army and navy, which, in 1870, comprised about 590,000,000 francs, and has to change her tariff and income taxes. France managed, during the reign of Napoleon III, to pay four milliards of francs—war expenses ; and when in the summer of 1868 she made a loan for army expenses, etc., and everybody anticipated a war with Prussia, which then only was prevented by the revolution which had broken out in Spain, said loan was signed thirty-four times. At the high rate of 69½ francs for three-francs bond, equivalent to 115 5-6 for five per cent., fully *fifteen milliards* were put at her disposal. It was, indeed, a speaking witness of the accumulated wealth of France. It is an historical fact. To this same extent it is deplorable that these milliards of France are nearly gone already. The *Pays* so stated it in the fall of the year (1870) as having been expended upon the war up to that time and until its end. It cited the figures :

1 milliard for armaments from 1868 to 1870.
1½   do.   for destroyed and rebuilding of fortifications.
1½   do.   for arms, and cannon, and other war materials, which the Germans have destroyed and taken as booty.
2   do.   for destruction of buildings, fields, and other immovable property, by both the French and their enemy.
1   do.   for complete and partial ruin of manufacturers, farmers, and speculators.

2½ milliards for payment to Germany for the cost of the war (which has since then been doubled by Bismarck).

2 do. for losses consequent upon the direct effect of all these misfortunes.

These figures are rather summarily taken, yet they may have come within the knowledge of the exchequer. At least Pouyer-Quertiers stated in June, 1871, after this war was ended, and the damage done could be somewhat less vaguely estimated, that loans had to be made to the figure of eight milliards. Then it has to be considered that at least fourteen counties in which the war waged could not produce any grain, and the remainder seventy-five had no hands left to do the work. Most of the manufacturers were equally stagnated. The harvest of 1870 had not been gathered in at all upon a large section of the country, and in other parts it was wilfully destroyed that it might not fall into the hands of the Germans; besides, was not a good one in consequence of insufficient rains. This want of grain, last year, has proved since then to have been severely felt, as could not be otherwise expected.

Another consideration is, that the rich had left the country, at least would be absent for a long while; in short, the non-republican conduct of waging war has added losses upon losses without necessity. As to the world, generally it does not admire at all heroism of bloodshed in any shape any longer. The days of Cæsarism are over, and the poet writes the epitaph:

>Cæsar Galliam subegit, Cæsar noster maximus,
>Castra fregit et Gallorum hostium exercitus,
>Fugans milites Suaves Gallicosque Zephyros.
>
>Imperator Germanorum, Cæsar noster maximus,
>Regnum fundat exoptatum, rem exoptatissimam
>Nobis adferens a flava Sequana in patriam.
>
>En Augustus imperator, Cæsar noster maximus,
>Fines auget Germanorum, quondam eheu! perditos,
>Lotharingi cum Alsatis redeunt in patrios.
>
>Ecce venit Triumphator, Cæsar noster maximus,
>Ecce venit in triumpho maximus exercitus,
>Ecce venit Pax triumphans, fructus noster aureus.

Unfortunately the proximity to each other of so many largely populated and warlike nations in Europe having made it indispensable for self-preservation to study the science of life destruction minutely, it has fortunately developed itself to a degree that it is not likely that war shall again be resorted to for purposes of settling political difficulties by it, as it borders upon the aboriginal character of cruelty.

As to the present war it demonstrates but the ancient principle of how to carry it on victoriously. The initiation or strategical independence is the main point. The genius of the commander-in-chief secures it to the army, holding it in readiness to commence operations sooner than his antagonist, and if at all possible, with a numerically stronger force. The Germans acted upon this principle, and the result has been astonishingly good and unprecedentedly successful. The French were always taken by surprise. All the German generals listened to but one voice: the King's of Prussia in grand command, with General Moltke as his immediate executive.

The French had Napoleon, and Napoleon had Leboeuf. Unfortunately, Napoleon resigned his command and placed it in the hands of two commanding generals instead of one, which proved ruinous.

The Germans quickly cutting Bazaine off Verdun and Thionville prevented his junction with McMahon, forcing the latter to capitulate. When Bazaine decided to retreat upon Verdun, he wasted forty-eight hours, as he had to return the same way, which enabled the Prussians to blockade his way. Equally slow McMahon approached Stenay, moving to and fro without covering his march at all. It is well known that the Germans at Saarbruecken as well as at Mars la Tour, were much weaker in point of numbers than the French, not having at all concentrated their strength; yet they conquered through mutual and timely assistance among each other during the fight—although Napoleon I used to say that two-thirds of success is the consequence of calculation, and but one-third luck; it appears that the Germans calculated all three-thirds the whole war through, not having lost a single battle. Fifty thousand cavalry covering at all times the armies, while preparing for battle as well as while marching, it cannot be said otherwise but that they carried out this plan methodically, which realized their victories. Wars carried on with the assistance of railroads, telegraphs and needle-guns, are almost new; at least the old Bulow system is exploded. Troops are transported three times quicker than before, and heavy war materials fifteen times. The French already in their Italian war in 1859, availed themselves of railroads. It appears that the destructive needle-gun and chassepots procrastinate the commencement of the fight. Bayonets and cavalry have changed their importance but little, except that the attack commences from far greater distances than before. The artillery aims 5,000 paces and ceases with 1,500, while formerly it commenced firing at 1,500 paces. And as to the mitrailleuse of the French, it has proved of little service. The dreaded French mitrailleuse requires as great a circumference as its organization is expensive and preparation costly, without even coming up to anything like the effect which the canon has in all collective points of consideration.

It likewise offers to the enemy's fire an equally large aim as the canon does. In firing at large distances it proves to be of little or no account, because its absolute capacity to hit is too deficient, the room it can command too small, and an observation almost impossible. Upon small distances the densely collected sharp-shooters of the enemy are as dangerous to it as to artillery in general. Towards troops behind covering, it cannot be used at all, because its shots have not the power to pierce nor to scatter. To initiate the offensive it cannot be used, and for defense, it can aid the infantry then only when the necessary room for the front is wanted in order to direct the sufficient number of rifles from a suitable position—for instance, in the defense of narrow mountain passes, etc. It is, therefore, very rare indeed that it can aid the infantry advantageously. These are the reasons which convince that canister shot will not be largely resorted to in future wars, as long as this sanguinary way of settling difficulties is at all tolerated by civilization.

Strange to say the terrific battles of the war of 1870, were, after all, less sanguinary than those of Borodino and Waterloo. The German loss at Gravelotte is estimated but at six per cent., and that of the French at eleven per cent., as the consequence of firing at very large distances. The so-called luck in war is now, fortunately, put into so small a compass, through knowledge, which includes the knowledge of the inhumanity and crime of war, that peace, which is the well applied knowledge of civilization, will soon conquer war to the only and true glory of sound sense as the element of knowledge. Thus, Germany, at least, being both physically and intellectually the domineering power on the continent of Europe, will force war back among nations that henceforth shall prove their semi-civilization by a reckless provocation to it. On the other hand, she will endeavor and succeed in a diplomatic way, conjointly with Great Britain and America, to pacify beforehand the temper of nations having differences to adjust, so that the tender growth of the proletariat of mankind into the social circle of gentility, as the grand object of civilization, may not be disturbed by wars any more. It cannot be heralded often enough throughout the world that wars are the consequence of a void in civilization on the part of the great masses of the population forming a nation, from which deplorable fact had sprung in ancient times the dire necessity of monarchial governments, which, in adjustment of the degree and nature of barbarity thus lawlessly practiced, and in consideration of the number of millions thus found barbarous, ruled autocratically. In proportion to the waning of barbarity in the millions of a nation the rigor is relaxed, and a constitutional government adopted, until the nation at large has altogether emancipated itself from every remnant of feudalism, and is able to govern itself, adopting the republican form of government.

Man then lives peaceably through the power of culture, and appreciates reveringly the sovereign power endowed with by the Creator for His inscrutable purpose of the human race at all existing upon earth; therefore, while so living to be personally independent, to live happily, and to act humanely. The republican government thus appears, and really is the clerkship of a nation, as composed of such an enlightened fraternity, of whom every one is supposed to avail himself of the full republican trust of personal independence to render himself through life better in virtues than he is, and the nation at large to progress the civilization of the age by socially developing their moral acts, and unitedly apply them.

On the other hand, how quickly a nation can recover from the shocks of a devastating war lasting four years, to-day the condition of the United States proves best. The victorious Union had to make loans to the amount of over $3,000,000. The quick recovery was made possible by immediately after the war reducing the expenses of the army and navy to the utmost extent. France, of course, is not as rich in resources, and capability of standing heavy losses, as the United States are. Although famous for its manufactures, yet the French people, like the remainder of European continental people, are rather necessitated to value money, the whole of Europe footing up as much land as is about arable in the United States of America.

When four years afterwards one of the most distinguished men of progress of this or any other age, Ex-Governor of California, Leland Stanford, planned the greatest technical enterprise of the day, a through railroad from the Atlantic to the Pacific, it became evident that the thinking, laboring people of the United States had forgotten all about the war. And if not so fast as the people of the United States, still the French will recover. Her national property will steadily reproduce itself in its principal sections. The French, with a vivaciousness of spirit rarely found, inhabiting a fertile country, although but as large as one single State among some odd thirty of the United States, the State of California, still its situation, the national character of the people, will soon forget the debt of five millards of francs, provided they follow the example of the United States, and disarm, as demanded by the principle of the republic, and then impose a very heavy import duty upon every superfluous article of luxury which the rich can stand and the poor don't care for.

The French national character has excellent qualifications. The French are sober, industrious, parsimonious, and singly very peaceable throughout the country—the clubs of Paris excepted. What is, therefore, understood by the word, "the people," these have found out by this time, through the pressure of debt, what is meant by bearing the incubus of royalty.

The idea of being dazzled by royal splendor in this age would show an Indian taste, as everybody knows that it is despotically maintained at the expense of the people, to the detriment of their ability to directly provide for themselves more comforts of their own choice, and deprives the nation from superintending the expenditure of such regal money for the benefit of all, in the manifold manner in which it is done in America.

But the pressure of debt will operate upon France; her economists shall attentively read J. Stuart Mill, the English national economist, or send over to Washington for information. France shall soon be out of debt. She shall be vigilant as to the Bourbons, Orleans, Napoleons, these so-called hereditary adherents to royalty. That there is a minority of benighted people left at all times, and in all civilized countries, who adhere to legends of such a past, is deplorably unalterable. These are like corn-flowers in a wheat field which has been ploughed and resown a dozen times; they are both of no account, simply beautiful to look at; the economist and farmer are accustomed to them. The Orleanists, it is vividly remembered, openly said: "France is rich enough to pay for her glory." What glory? The glory of ambition and of conquest—the crime of murderous wars. A nice glory in the face of reason and America!! of civilization and of practically applied common sense!—an inadmissible theory—an exploded practice! France is now fully convinced that wars are non-republican, wicked, and belong to mediæval times and ungovernable people. This war did it. Sebastopol, Syria, China, and Mexico were not enough, nor the splendor of the metropolis could hide the cripples in the glare of the sun of day, nor the neglect of the thousands of the needy. But now the French Republic, having proved by the overthrow of the rebellion that by far the greatest number of the population of the country are aware of the danger that is consequent upon rebellion, and more so from aristocrats who created rebellion, by not educating the poor, they will, in the face of the five millards of francs which their last doings levied upon them all, take good care that it does not reoccur. They shall not listen to chauvinists who harangue a republican country with retaliation. The nation will know how to put into the legislative body men universally respected and carefully voted for, who are enlightened, and consequently peaceably inclined, and industrious, producing citizens withal, and who, as such, put out of the way the old seductive budget of the army and navy, reducing it, like in America, to a reasonable and legitimate standard. Taking America as an example, where a President of the United States receives $25,000 per annum, because he would feel hurt if the country, the people, should be forced, on account of his position, to support him as if he was a cripple, and not a worthy man, the worthiest of them all, in their own judgment, who labors and is happy to do his duty to the country at all times, which, like the religion of man, is rewarded from within and not without. The French should now make a law which prohibits the exchequer to be drawn upon for war purposes, it being then to rescue native-born citizens from incarceration while traveling, like the English nobly did it in Abyssinia, the Americans lately in Corea, China, and in this war the Germans memorably repulsed the French. Such wars are in their nature necessary in this age—lawful constabulary proceedings. They rest on a different principle altogether; it is simply self-defense, like the Union of America defended itself against rebellion, any nation against invasion, man against a murderer, or the exercise of force is used in the maintenance of law. How often do we hear people in Europe exclaiming: "Life is not safe in a republic!" the idea as if they could not reasonably comprehend that life is everywhere safe if man takes care of himself first. It is little credit to a man, and looks very suspicious in a nation, to ask a gens d'arms to do it for him. A gentleman includes the guarantee to himself, through his gentlemanly behavior, that he has no enemies, and that consequently his life is safe.

Besides there are far more robbers, etcetra, bad people in a monarchical country than in a republic, on account of abject poverty: the consequence of a lack of social freedom to enable man to better his condition himself, and so perfect himself in the legitimate exercise of his individual sovereignty, which is his right.

One of the weightiest reasons of all, which can predict to the republic of France a speedy recovery from the calamities of war, is the utter void of retaliation on the part of the Germans during this war guaranteeing to France no unnecessary disturbance in future, which concerns her. The republic knows well that public opinion best shields it against foreign aggression, but if ever it should prove weak, and allow an attempt at overwhelming and overthrowing the republic to be successfully made a third time culminating in royalty, which signifies war against Germany, then Germany shall demand full pay of the old score of 1806 and 1808, and in proportion to the following figures: If 4,500,000 Prussians who inhabited a piece of territory after the peace of Tilsit as concluded by Napoleon I, of 2,856 square German miles were obliged to pay to the French nation; thalers, 245,000,000, Prussian currency, how much, shall 35,500,000, or more of French people have to pay, in land and money, who live upon such a date of the declaration of war against Germany, upon a piece of territory exclusive of colonies of just about 200,000 (English) square miles? A fresco painting with an appropriate inscription, should immediately adorn the tribunal of the presidential chair, in the legislative hall at Paris, that the solution to the above Pythagorean problem may paralize the effort of any member there who shall intend to annul the republic !

France now dutifully takes every surplus franc; firstly, to educate the million, and, further, expends it upon the proletariat in comfortable abodes, after the Peabody plan, and lawfully and carefully looks after it. France does it in a truly charitable, republican manner, and so should all Europe.

The houses for the inebriates should be all over Europe multiplied, and the river Styx dammed off, the waters of which are intoxicating beverages, which infuriate. The latter mammothian enterprise will set millions to work, for the river Styx overflows the whole of paradise upon earth, fertilizing in it the domain of Satan Sin. As among civilized nations the Americans are the most industrious people, among mankind the Chinese, and of all creation the bees, nature so proves by its love of labor the superiority: of the one in universal individual comfort; the other, one-third of all mankind, in the comparative freedom from vice; and the third, by the accumulation of honey, which puts at all times to shame the labor of the most industrious man. Our dreadful ignorance of the Chinese language, debared us, hitherto-fore, from estimating properly those 400,000,000 of living people, but the time is at hand, since steam girdles the world, when civilized nations may learn a great deal of them, as they constantly do of nature. Besides the English and the Americans, the French republic has the best chance, thanks to the acquisition of those six provinces in Anam (Cochin-China), which are theirs, to reimburse the nation for the outlay, at the time of what was intended not to reach all, like in a republic, but be absorbed by the Napoleonic dynasty.

PART THE ELEVENTH.

PEACE.—THE NEW BOUNDARY OF GERMANY.

After the capture of Napleon III at Sedan, and the flight of the Regency from Paris, Germany found herself in a dilemma of the most serious kind. She saw nobody with whom to conclude peace. With whom, therefore, was an idle question, because it could not be answered. Germany was ready to make peace, asking nothing but security for the impossibility of France to ever again rise in the offensive against Germany, as well as for the covering of the costs of the war. Napoleon, in spite of his captivity, was yet the legitimate head of the nation; the latest legitimate expressions of the will of the French people, the plebiscitum of May, 1870, had not been canceled nor revoked. The Legislative Body and the Senate, though by force dispersed on the 4th of September, could not be considered as having been sent away by the nation; on the other hand the Provisional Government of the Republic existed, acknowledged, at least, by the majority of the people. *De facto* it had no legal basis to rest upon, because the French nation at large had not been consulted in regard to sanctioning it. Germany therefore reserved to herself, Napoleon, or his Regency, to make peace with; or again, with the Legislative Body of France, or with the party of national defense, respectively: with a committee so authorized by France to conclude peace. Napoleon, therefore, was treated at Wilhelmshohe not as a prisoner, but as a fugitive Emperor, at the same time that Favre was admitted to the German head-quarters soliciting to negotiate for an armistice and convoke a provisional government. The latter attempt was given up at the end of September, a second time at the end of October, when Thiers had returned from his visit to the various neutral governments of Europe, and was formally introduced by them to the French nation as the proper person who, and with whom, peace could be negotiated. He came, introduced by monarchs, but not by the republic of France. However, the government of national defence, organizing new armies and sending them to Paris, preferred a sort of dictature to both Theirs and peace. They intentionally evaded a national representation of the will of the people. At last negotiations were cut off altogether, which was surely not the fault of the Germans.

This dictature must have believed in the ultimate success of the battles, and so the war was resumed.

Matters remained *in statu quo* until the armies were everywhere defeated, and Paris could not be saved.

At that time, about the end of January, 1871, Germany might as well have taken Paris and its forts, made 180,000 prisoners, disarmed the national guards, occupied the town and forts, assumed the custody over the exchequer of France, and introduced the police into the clubs. All that was possible and executable after monarchical maxims generally, but the original question, with whom to make peace? what finishes the war? remained unanswered. In that case, as just now mentioned, peace could not be concluded with the provisional government. The government a prisoner—as Napoleon had been made one at Sedan—had no authority to negotiate for peace. In Bordeaux Gambetta continued war; he would indeed have continued it until all France would have had to be occupied by the Germans, and even then the question could not have been answered, with whom to negotiate peace. Of Napoleon, the Germans could not think any longer, nor of his Regency, as both had lost every influence in France ever since September, 1870. The Napoleons were indeed consigned to oblivion by the French nation.

Germany, instead of taking and occupying Paris, found, nevertheless, the way to make peace. The provisional government in Paris had not to be disturbed, that was the idea. It could not possibly be accomplished. It had to be so managed that the provisional government, which was well aware of the necessity on its part to make peace, had to so conduct itself that the war party should respect it, and then take measures for an election all over France, which should lead to a new national government. That by it peace would be arrived at, was expected as natural. The armistice of the 28th of January was, therefore, an important step towards it. It saved Germany the trouble of transporting 180,000 prisoners to Germany, and the pacification and support of the excited Parisians, which their own government enjoyed. Another advantage was that the neutral powers could be convinced of the moderation of Germany, and its earnest desire for peace. Already Gambetta ceased his warcry; early in February the elections took place, and proved, as was duly predicted, a large majority in favor of peace. A chief of the executive was appointed by the national assembly, the first legitimate government since the 4th of September, who, imbued with the necessity to make peace, duly negotiated at German head-quarters for it, and signed the document accepted by the national assembly at Bordeaux. The preliminaries of peace were solemnly and mutually ratified at head-quarters, on the 2nd of March, and the answer to the query found and given.

From these preliminaries to the "definitive peace," was not an easy matter to proceed, by any means, and not expected by either party on the 26th of February, when the preliminaries were settled, that it would be so difficult to bring peace about. In France existed a lawful assembly, and a government accordingly. Nobody could foresee what pretensions might be made on the 18th of March, to question the rights of the national assembly and its executive of government to make peace. The case was strangely exceptional: indeed without example in history. And still there arose one. It was the Paris commune. Still stranger the revolution spread in quarters of Paris within range of the north and east forts, occupied by the Germans. The danger of this rebellion was the possibility that the conduct of the metropolis might be imitated in other large cities of France; then again, the great weakness and helplessness of the government with which Germany had concluded peace ; likewise the consequences of the possibility of a successful rebellion, or one so partially as it, would affect the exchequer of France by retarding the financial and economical growth of it, of interest to Germans at that moment. As to Germany, she kept perfectly quiet ; the Germans had nothing to do with internal French quarrels. Besides, another difficulty arose, from another direction: the French government, though anxious to conclude peace as quickly as possible, and to be on good terms with Germany, exerted itself to postpone the conferences at Brussels rather than push them. Doubts arose after all whether they could or would be in favor of peace. The German empire had no representative at Versailles who might have found out and informed the country of the true cause of this vascillation. The situation was to such a degree delicate and perplexing that the Germans were about to take Paris without further ado, and keep it as a pledge until the French should bend to the necessity of making peace. Bismarck, however, adroitly managed the difficulty. He hit upon the expedient of personally confronting the French ministers, and succeeded admirably. He soon found out that the difficulty rested on a misunderstanding. Not only did he find the French ministers at Frankfort quite tractable, determined to make peace, and as quickly as possible, and by no means bashful as to acknowledging the truth: that France could very well afford to pay so just a sum of money. Whether it was a change of climate which invigorated their manliness, or the absence of English advice and mediators, or the Bismarckian eloquence which created the lovely harmony between them, it is hard to tell. Enough that the French ministers at Frankfort were found to be entirely different genii than were the negotiators at Brussels. They even decided to still further secure the money which had been in the proclamation agreed upon to be paid. The first half milliard should be paid thirty days after the capitulation of Paris, the second payment of 1000 millions to be paid during 1871, and then only Germans to quit the forts of Paris. By the 4th of May, 1872, the fourth half milliard should have to be paid. All payments to be made in coin or notes on good banks, and first-class bills of exchange. As to the remaining milliards to be produced, the stipulated time, as given in the preliminaries, should be adhered to.

The occupation of the forts of Paris until one and a half milliards should have been paid by the end of 1870, was considered absolutely indispensable and necessary as a matter of precaution against fluctuations, to which the internal condition of France at that time remained exposed. In regard to the treaty of commerce, when it is part of the financial system, and forms one of the most important portions of indirect taxation, Germany took the firm ground that it should not be forced upon a great nation. The working classes, as they now contemplate the matter in spite of the episode of free trade during the reign of Napoleon, would feel constantly chafed at Germany being at all favored by the tariff. Suffice it for Germany that the reduction in the tariff, and similar advantages which France has accorded to Great Britain, Belgium, Holland, Switzerland, Austria, and Russia, should continue to be accorded to Germany also. The extraordinary favors above this, as accorded to the Zolverein in 1862, would, however, be canceled. It does not matter much to Germany, for France has always been slow to make concessions. At one time France wished to cancel all the above named treaties of commerce, the one of Germany included; whether it can now afford to so do, remains to be seen.

THE PRELIMINARIES OF PEACE.

The preliminaries of peace, as stipulated at Versailles, on the 26th of February, 1871, were worded as follows:

Between the Chancellor of the German Empire,
Count Otto von Bismarck-Schönhausen,
who holds power of attorney from the Emperor of Germany and King of Prussia,
The Minister of Foreign Affairs of the King of Bavaria,
Count Otto von Bray-Steinburg,
The Minister of Foreign Affairs of the King of Wurtemburg,
Freiherrn August von Waechter,

The Minister of State and President of the Ministerial Council of
the Grand Duchy of Baden, Julius Jolly, Esq.,
all of whom represent the German Empire
on the one side,
And the Chief of the Executive Power of the French Republic,
Monsieur Thiers,
And the Minister of Foreign Affairs, Jules Favre,
who represent France,
on the other side;

(the power of attorney of all being found in good and regular form correct,) is made the following agreement, which shall serve as the preliminary basis to peace, to be ratified later (and which was duly concluded at Frankfort-on-the-Main, on the 10th of May, 1871).

ARTICLE I. France resigns to Germany all her rights and pretentions to those territories which lie to the east of the boundary, which is sketched as follows : The line of demarcation commences on the northwesterly boundary of the Canton Cattenom, stretching towards the Grand Duchy of Luxemburg, continues southward to the western boundary of the Cantons Cattenom and Thionville, divides the Canton Briey, while running lengthways of the western boundaries of the parishes of Montois-la Montagne and Roncourt, as well as lengthways of the eastern boundaries of the parishes of Marie-aux Chenes, Saint Ail, and Habouville, touches the boundary line of the Canton Gorze, which it divides lengthway of the boundaries of the parishes Vionville, Bouxieres and Onville, runs parallel to the southwest respectively, the south frontier of the County of Metz, the western boundary of the County Chateau-Salins, as far as the parish Pettoncourt, of which line it embraces the western and southern frontier, and then follows the spur of hills which stretch between the Seille and the Moncel, as far as the frontier of the County of Saarburg, south of Garde. Then the line of demarcation unites at the frontier of this county as far as the County Tanconville, of which it touches the northern boundary. From there it follows the spurs of hills which are situated between the sources of the rivulets Sarreblanche and of the Vezouze, as far as the boundary of the Canton Schirmeck, continues along the western frontier of said canton, includes the parishes of Saales, Bourg-Bruche, Colroy-la-Roche, Plaine, Ranrupt, Saulxures, and Saint Blaise-la-Roche, all of which are within the Canton Saales, and then joins the western boundary of the provinces of Lower and Upper Rhine, as far as the Canton Belfort. Quitting the southern boundary of it, not far from Vourvenans, it divides the Canton Delle at the southern frontier of the parishes Bourogne and Froide-Fontaine, and so reaches the frontier of Switzerland, running along the eastern boundaries of the parishes of Jonchery and Delle.

The German Empire shall, forever, possess these boundaries in full sovereign power and right of ownership to same. An international commission, consisting on both sides, in equal numbers, of the representatives of the contracting parties, shall immediately be ordered, after exchange of ratifications of the present treaty, to arrange upon the spot the new boundary line in accordance with the aforesaid stipulation.

Said Commision shall govern the division of ground and soil, as well as divide the value of property which heretofore belonged in common to districts and parishes, which now are separated by the new boundary line. In case of differences of opinion among themselves in regard to the boundary line, and the orders for their settlement, said Commissioners shall refer the matter to their respective Governments for ultimate decision.

The boundary line, fixed as above delineated, is given in green upon the new map, of which two have been made, which are exactly alike, and show the territorial sections which come under the Government of Alsace, as published already in September, 1870, at Berlin, by the geographical and statistical department of the War Office. The two maps shall be affixed, one to each of the documents of the present treaty.

The line of demarcation as so far given, has, however, been changed as by mutual agreement of the contracting parties, and altered as follows: In the former department of Moselle the villages Marie-aux Chenes, near St. Privat-la-Montagne and Vionville, to the west of Rezonville, are ceded to Germany, against which France shall keep the town and forts of Belfort, with some city property attached to it, which shall later be fixed upon.

ARTICLE II. France shall pay to the Emperor of Germany the sum of five milliards of francs. At least one milliard of which shall be paid in the course of the year 1871, and the remainder in the course of three years from the date of the ratification of the present treaty.

ARTICLE III. The evacuation of the French from territory taken possession of by German troops shall commence after the ratification of the present treaty by the National Assembly in session at Bordeaux. Immediately after the ratification, the German troops shall quit the city limits of Paris, as well as those forts of Paris which are situated upon the left bank of the River Seine. The Germans shall likewise evacuate in as little time as possible, according to agreement between the military authorities of both countries, the departments altogether of Calvados, Orne, Sarthe, Eure et Loire, Loiret, Loir et Cher, Indre et Loire, and Yonne; and further, the departments Seine inferieure, Eure, Seine et Oise, Seine et Marne, Aube, Cote d'or, down to the left bank of the Seine. At the same time the French troops shall withdraw to beyond the Loire, which river they shall not be permitted to cross ere the treaty of definite peace is signed. Excepted is the garrison of Paris, the strength of which shall not exceed 40,000 men, and those garrisons which are absolutely necessary to be maintained for the security of fortified places.

The evacuation by German troops of departments which are situated between the right bank of the Seine and the eastern boundary, shall gradually take place after the ratification of the definitive treaty of peace has been signed, and the payment of the first half milliard of contribution money shall have been duly made, as stipulated in Article II.

The evacuation shall commence from those departments which lie nearest to Paris, and shall so continue in proportion to the contribution money coming in. After the first payment of half a milliard, the following departments shall be evacuated : Somme, Oise, and those sections of the departments Seine inferieure, Seine et Oise, and Seine et Marne, which are situated upon the right bank of the Seine, as well as the sections of the Department Seine, and the forts upon the right bank of the Seine.

After the payment of two milliards, the occupation of French territory by German troops shall comprise but the departments of Marne, Ardennes, Haute Marne, Meuse, Vosges, Meurthe, as well as the fortress Belfort, with its city limits, which shall serve as further pledge for the debt until the remainder three milliards shall have been forthcoming. The number of German troops upon said territory shall not exceed 50,000 men.

It is left for the Emperor of Germany to decide whether he will accept a financial guaranty to a territorial one, which he has got now, while occupying certain sections of France, should the Government of France make overtures to that effect for the purpose of a riddance of the Germans from France, and the Emperor of Germany prefer accepting them as in the interest of Germany as amounting to the same thing.

For the three milliards, if their payment should be put off, five per cent. interest will be added to the sum total until paid, and counted from the day of ratification of the present compact.

ARTICLE IV. The German troops shall not touch anything in the departments which they occupy, in the way of requisitions, whether of money or property, of the French. Against which those troops who have to remain in France for the present shall be maintained at the expense of the Government of France, and provided for at a ratio as shall be agreed upon by the Commissary Department of the German Empire.

ARTICLE V. The interests of the inhabitants of territory ceded by France to Germany, shall be regulated for them as favorably as possible, in regard to their commerce and industrial rights, and as soon as the conditions of a definitive peace shall have been fixed upon. For this purpose a certain time will be agreed to, within which those inhabitants shall enjoy especial facilities for a free exchange of their commercial productions of industry. The German Government shall not hinder the free egress of inhabitants from those sections of territory, nor shall it take measures towards any of those inhabitants which touch the person or property.

ARTICLE VI. The prisoners of war who have not as yet been liberated, by way of an exchange of prisoners, shall be delivered up immediately upon the ratification of the preliminaries. In order to facilitate the transportation of the French prisoners, the French government shall put a certain number of railway cars at the disposal of the German authorities, and send so many of them into the interior of Germany as shall be found expedient for such an accommodation and at a charge the same as paid in France by the Government for the transport of the military.

ARTICLE VII. The opening of the negotiations in regard to a definitive peace, which is to be concluded upon the basis of these preliminaries, shall take place in Brussels, and without delay, after ratification of their contents by the National Assembly and the Emperor of Germany.

ARTICLE VIII. After conclusion and ratification of the definitive peace, the administration of the departments which have to remain occupied by German troops, shall again be turned over to French authorities. Yet the latter shall have to submit to the dictation of commanding generals of those German troops in regard to what they consider necessary to be required of said authorities for the safety, the care, and the cantonments of soldiers.

In the departments so occupied the collecting of taxes shall be attended to after ratification of the present treaty for account of the French Government and through French officials.

ARTICLE IX. It is understood that the present treaty stipulations cannot give to the German military authorities a right of any kind to the ownership of those sections of the territory, which are not at present occupied by German troops.

ARTICLE X. The present preliminaries shall be laid without delay before the Emperor of Germany, as well as before the French National Assembly, which holds its sessions at Bordeaux, for ratification. (Signatures.)

Done at Versailles the 26th of February, 1871.
Witness: BLUME,
        Mayor in the staff of Generals.

PART THE TWELFTH.

GERMANY AT HOME.

At home Germany has now laws, thanks to progress, which give freedom to the press, that man may promulgate his opinion and cultivate truth, knowledge and taste among the people—give liberty to marry by pacifying the old feudal anxiety of caste, so mainly and obviously detrimental to nuptial bliss of the parties concerned—does away with the uncharitable act of imprisonment for debt, which debars man from rallying his energies thus paralized, while it lulls the other into inertness to look out for his own business, whom to trust and when losing, is apt to blame everybody else save himself, in spite of the law shielding him in the courts of justice against downright villainy—secures free labor, and finally regulates trade and commerce among the divers States of the Union; provides for the homeless, the sick and the needy in a dutiful and suitable way, and in a fraternal christian manner.

How greatly and beneficially these aforesaid laws affect personal liberty, advance the unrestrained movements of man, and above all, lift the working classes into home comforts through these laws, which secure their happiness and shield their independence, enabling them to put a proper value upon their labor and time, and thus receive far better wages than hithertofore attainable according to their labor's legitimate worth, all these traits of civilization cannot be loudly enough commended and applauded, nor by the Germans sufficiently heartily appreciated.

That Germany has so changed for the better, within comparatively a brief space of time, is perfectly wonderful, and what is still more gratifying, the world believes in it as having been proved by success, and correctly and justly attributes the defeat of the French, not to a decadence of prowess in the latter nation, but simply to the greater moral and intellectual strength of Germany as displayed by the Union.

Those mental links of theirs, composed of the strength of enlightenment, which were commenced to be made a generation previously to

1870, have now been hotly smelted in the unearthly fire of the war by all concerned, and have completed the chain of brotherhood to a length which shall maintain its solidity of independence forever. It shall be extended to the outside world, until the last German now under foreign monarchial rule shall belong to the mother country, and the change of the present form of Government into the republican be duly, peaceably, and everlastingly inaugurated.

This latter task of the requisition of foreigners shall comparatively be an easy one, and it is to be hoped will be a peaceful one.

Instead of 40,000,000, as at present, Germany shall then foot up about 60,000,000 population, a strength which is at all times of the future a guarantee for peace, as long as monarchial governments addicted to wars shall be in Europe ; but at the same time points to the impossibility of harmonizingly holding together so vast an enlightened nation, except under a republican form of Government, after the experience in the United States of America.

How petty monarchies wane under such auspices this war has best shown. As the previous alienation of the South from the North was the work of unscrupulous machinations, therefore unenlightened, so it had to wane before the power of genius of a Bismarck, and the patriotism of an Emperor William and his son.

Some thirty kingdoms, dukedoms, principalities, free cities, etcetera, German sovereignties, among one kindred people, upon a small piece of land of the globe, harrassing one another by wanton obstreperousness, to love each other as nearest relatives among mankind, suddenly concentrating into one national government in Germany. What progress of the age !

What is it which so blessed their understanding ?—tearing the grey veil from their eyes, and showed them cured of glaucoma, with no fear of a relapse? It was the universally applied medicine of the school book ! ! ! Religion, faith in God and themselves, as evoked upon the occasion by the hostility of a warlike and aggressive nation—self-defense in barbarous times, made necessary to be deplored.

It lead to the internal application of knowledge, instead of the use of the painful and risky operations of external force. And who is the learned physician, the Graeffe of the faculty? America ! America ! where 8,000,000 of citizens of German origin continually correspond with their respective relatives on the continent of Europe, and tell them how freely, unrestrainedly, and comfortably they live and are happy.*

---

* The poorer of the means of subsistence foreigners arrive in America, the more gratefully and quicker will they write home, provided always, and applicable to all nations alike, the individual has temperate habits; but the richer the universal foreigner arrives in America, the longer the time in which he improves to comprehend

As to this war, if there is anything which could at all recompense a citizen for having bravely risked his life to save the country, outside of the reward, with which his conscience of having done his duty fills his breast with serene happiness, it is for once the undisguised, straightforward intention on the part of the Germans to amend their social laws—and what is more, they have done it.

There now exists a universal right and liberty of a citizen of one State desirous of choosing and settling in any other German State, to so do, and to be viewed in every respect as if he were born there. It is altogether in imitation of America; it is completely republican, humane, and broad. The citizen so settling has free liberty to do what he may please in pursuit of his happiness; he has the same state rights as the citizen born there, can settle permanently, labor as he may prefer, can apply for some official position, can buy and sell land, can become, as said before, a citizen, if he chooses, of that State; in fact, stands on a par with one born there, including every justice in courts, which is eked out to him as to others, and every juridical protection. Neither the State where he was born in, or came from last, nor any other, can molest him, while in his new domicil

---

this incomparably free country. The latter gentlemen, from Dan to Bethsheba, alight at their respective clubs and stay there, adding nothing to their knowledge, nor do they forget what afflicted them in Europe with the glaucoma upon their vision; they absolutely defy, above everything, the appreciation of the virtue of labor in any shape, which necessarily consigns them to the more arduous duties of the refinement of the aboriginal, in the various shapes of sensual gratification more or less gross. They are the unrelenting enemies of the charitable feeling of brotherhood and tolerance, until introduced to members of the club, having excited their curiosity by their good breeding, their knowledge and their wealth.

Upon becoming more intimately acquainted, the Europeans begin to reflect, and are beyond measure astonished to find that their new *conge'*, the Americans, are the beloved sons of self-made men, and their amiability, unresisting, because natural in the atmosphere of this country, and the Americans, that the ancestors of the foreigners of rank slew more human beings in battle than the King of Ashantee, and the "accomplished gentleman" generally an icy matter of form.

It is this incorrigible restraint, fostered by a want of productive labor, and aggrivated by aristocratic customs, which prevents an intelligent *foreigner* from comprehending the moral strength and vastness of the number of useful and important citizens in the United States to their real worth, and actually leaves the country with a theatrical impression upon his mind that the liberty of America is a gaudy *coulisse*, behind which the tragedy of pandemonium is rehearsed, which is bound to swallow up the Union with fire and brimstone, when the country shall be as populated as Europe.

It is well that he leaves, and better still, should he be accompanied by a precious bevy of promiscuous infidels, who, born Christians, have lost their pious faith in God, in the permanency of the Republican institutions, and in marriage. Setting aside the reprehensible tendency in a purely patriotic view, such harrangue, at this age, from otherwise intelligent people, to which one is unavoidably subjected, is, to say the least, extremely vulgar, and would deserve no notice whatever if it was not

and abode. This law, so generous, humane, and republican, came into force 1st July, 1871. All the States of the Union embraced it except Bavaria, and that State is, of course, but for the present reluctant to so do.

It comprises not only laboring men, mechanics, and merchants, but every citizen. As it is of more general avail among persons in the habit of constantly moving about, it is so much more beneficial in a public point of view. This great law answers the modern principles of social rights, it does away with the old barrier of sedentary habits and hereditary customs, cures the lethargic effects of home sickness, and hurls every one into the great current of public usefulness and cheerful labor. Soon the country will be too small, and they want colonies. Go ahead. If that law is not copied from America, then the members of the German Diet are men of sound republican principles, beyond a doubt, and are, indeed, original, and deserve encomium far and wide. With this great law the last fibre of a narrow-minded, selfish, particularismus is outrooted.

As it is in the Union of America, so it is in Germany: A citizen of California is as dear to the Union of America as a citizen of Maine or Florida; and in Germany a citizen of Prussia is as integral a part of the Union of Germany to-day as is one of Saxony or Wurtemberg. All this was planned in 1866, and in four years fully consummated. What a progress!

---

positively dangerous to public welfare because of its contamination among the unsophisticated.

To openly rattle at pillars of the civilization of ages, built and hourly strengthened by reason, truth and duty, fully sustained by grateful experience, and resting eternally erected upon the living truth of life itself, cannot but end in an entire overthrow of the mind of such an unfortunate individual, ultimately consigning it either to the asylum, or a paroxism of suicidal despair.

The fact is, the rich European seeks America in large cities only, just as he erroneously judges France from Paris only, mistaking the dash of extreme fashion for the governing principle of civilization, and therefore remains ignorant of the importance of the nation at large.

To an aristocrat the definition of the word materialismus is at all times wanted. His intellect is perfectly obfuscated as to the purposes of labor and its virtuous tendencies towards the advancement of the morality and happiness of man, as he never experienced the pecuniary necessity of it. He therefore cannot comprehend that to a civilized being, to the most civilized nation, there is nothing left but labor to save them, rich or poor, from idiocy or barbarism.

How can such minds comprehend the wealth which freedom in America lavishes upon every one worthy of himself, and enables him to make labor of all kinds, at all times, immediately productive and useful to himself and mankind at large. The sweets of toil, the charms of fraternity, are pitifully lost to the aristocrat, the ignorance of which sours his temper and makes him disagreeable to, and frequently derided by all enlightened fellow-men, all because inertness debarred him from knowing himself.

It appears from the broadness of this blessed law that it will become entirely unnecessary for Germany to forcibly insist upon the transfer of the not-united, monarchically ruled Germans; suffice that it becomes known abroad. The respective foreign governments will be obliged to initiate the question themselves, and meet Germany half way upon the subject, or else expect a revolution in their own countries which would lose them the provinces without remuneration.

As a matter of course, these various laws which the German Diet have so honestly made, were vouchsafed by the constitution ! To carry out the constitution is to guarantee liberalism and prepare for republicanism. It shows the spirit of the Union as being largely and equally diffused among the more uniformly enlightened people, which shall henceforth enable the nation to progress steadily and without hinderance by foreign nations, being at all times in a position to ignore with patriotic contempt any outside design at an impediment to such a steady national growth, correctly judged by them as emanating from a political jealousy, and the daring of the attempt itself at such a hostile act, to be sternly viewed in the light of a *casus belli*.

Those aforesaid intelligent classes shall continue to enlarge themselves from the million, just like in the United States of America, constantly reaching the surface of intellectual strength through as much universally uniform a school system as ever possibly to continue to be created, in order to be enabled to pave their own way to the notice of their merits in after life, by the fellow-citizens of their country and the world at large.

PART THE THIRTEENTH.

THE FUTURE OF THE GERMANIC RACE.—THE REGENERATION OF THE NETHERLANDS.

All that Germany needs besides the inland Germans, ruled over by foreigners, is Holland, its fleet and colonies, as it would give to the entire German Union the necessary adjacent seacoast to unitedly develop itself from, and to be enabled to create and maintain commercial facilities in proportion to its political greatness. Germany may then consider herself internationally independent, and in a position to enjoy freedom, happiness and influence in a full cosmopolitan view. Without Holland, the trans-oceanic commerce of Germany could never develop itself in due and full proportion to her national strength in general, and would unavoidably fall a prey to other nations, to the obvious detriment of her political influence.

As to the two only cosmopolitan nations of the World, the United States of America and Great Britain, they would conjointly receive the youthful giant with open arms, the only one besides them that was needed to vest the progress of future ages principally in the Germanic race. As there is room enough in Oceanica and Africa for the youthful giant to colonize among the natives, Germany does not interfere with the interests of Great Britain; on the contrary, the two nations shall progress together. The comparatively slumbering energy of the Dutch and Hanse-towns would revive to a miraculous extent under the strong shield of protection from the all-common fatherland. There never was a theory which could so easily be practically applied. The idea of the French, an inferior nation as to population when compared with Germany, as it should be, can be, and must be, to settle in Cochin-China! It would be an everlasting opprobrium to Germany to now not unite all her elements for a similar purpose. What glory it would be to civilization! What a future for Holland!

Why! she would by far eclipse Prussia in Germany. Holland in Germany would represent Germany in the world, while Prussia alone can represent the present Union but in Europe only, possessing neither colonies nor a fleet in adequate proportion to the present consolidation of the country. Holland, together with the Hanse-towns and Baltic ports, would lead the way into the world, converting once more their own commerce into uncountable gold, and the united productions of such a Germany into requisition by all mankind.

Holland and Belgium, (the lower lands of Germany, as formerly continental Germany formed the upper land of the Dutch Empire) have shown to the world in ages past what progress a nation can pave when possessing accessible and good harbors, and what a union of energetic men is capable of performing and achieving. Just like her incomparable neighbor in Europe to-day : the British nation. What has made Great Britain great? Character, knowledge of geography, indomitable courage, perseverance and discretion. Has she not got the same attributes ? Enough, Holland has proved it once, and shall prove it again. Those same virtues that gave her neighbor a London, a Liverpool, a Manchester, a Birmingham, a Glasgow, and a Calcutta, gave to the Netherlands of that great Dutch Empire an Amsterdam, a Rotterdam, a Middleburg, a Batavia, and to the now called Belgium an Antwerp, which was, about three centuries ago, the largest commercial city upon the globe. Imperishable as her renown is the one of Hamburg, Bremen, and Lubeck, which sisterhood shall again produce a cosmopolitan greatness, and undoubtedly greater than before, because assisted by steam.

As to Belgium, which is partially hidden from the German Union by the French language, the British Empire has hithertofore gladly protected her against the encroachments of France as entirely owing to the previous incompetency of Germany, on account of its distraction so to do, but which is now obviated by this war. The Belgians, as early as the fifteenth century, were proud to call themselves of Germanic origin. Her alienation, like that of Holland, is, therefore, unnatural, and, consequent only, upon the rise of the British Empire as having superseded the greatness of the Dutch Empire, from which dissolution the Netherlands were saved.

As Holland once included Germany, so shall Germany now include Holland, because, as said before, a great Union has to require a great seacoast. The re-establishment of the greatness of the Netherlands, and Hanse-towns, depends, therefore, entirely upon the entrance of the former into the present Union of Germany. The world will believe in it, because it remembers that the Wallonian city of Luttich vied in elegance with any other of the period—that the Luxemburgians afforded princes who ascended the throne of Germany, as well as that the memorable battle of Muehldorf decided the fate of Germany and Italy—that it was in Flanders where the German Hansa lived her imperishable renown before the world, and that Brugge was unsurpassed.

The most palmy days of Brabant where those when her people commingled their interests with those of the German Empire. As to the Vlamish people, those are of Germanic origin, best proved by the Vlamish language. They should all belong to Germany, with the exception, perhaps, of the Wallonians, who have, more or less, adopted French habits and customs ; in fact, are partially identified with the French.

How great the change has been among the two greatest nations of the world—the United States of America and Great Britain—in their esteem for the present German Union, and all the exemplary intelligent men who have so signally contributed to it is but seen here from the sudden silence of the sneering tongue among the vast forty millions, pardonably doubting at the commencement of the war victory over the French, although somewhat prepared for it since the battle of Sadowa, yet by no means expecting it as a certainty—said tongue became more and more paralized during the continuancy of the war and its endless victories. It ceased altogether from one end of the country to the other to audily vibrate, when by the venerable Emperor's entrance into Paris, the strange fact of the existence of a larger and stronger nation upon the continent of Europe than the French were, revealingly flashed upon them all at once, having become a glaringly incontrovertible and undeniable fact.

From the day that the Hollandish Knickerbockers had settled in New York, down to the hour in which the battle of Jena had lately been balanced in Paris by the above symbol of justice, the Americans at large had fancied the German to be a degenerated Hollander, the so-called Germany being incomprehensible to them on account of the confusion of petty sovereignties and feudal enmities among a kindred people, who were to them therefore excusably less known than the tribes of Indians upon their Occident.

The less educated again down to the altogether unceremonious boy, indulged even in epithets, which though law and inhospitable, had likewise their origin in the political nonentity of the Germans as a nation of union, of harmony, and of strength, not having had, until the battle of Sadowa, a single proof to the contrary on record, nor at all caring to investigate causes.

Although the present Germany is not as yet by any means what Holland once was—a cosmopolitan nation, and at her time the most powerful nation upon the globe, because of not having either colonies or a fleet in proportion to her continental greatness to-day—still America begins, as well as England, to expect it. As Holland once included Germany upon reasons of compactness, so Germany must now include Holland, her colonies and fleet.

It is the new doctrine of the concentration of nationalities practically carried out by monarchs, in order to save to the people not merely the expense of so many hereditary superfluities, but to legitimately centralize their power to suit the times, which demand on the part of a people, the expansion of general progress in proper accordance with this age of fleetness, which intends to exhaust the wealth of the world ever since Steam has brought it within reach of all.

If the Kings of Prussia, of Bavaria, of Saxony, of Hanover, of Wurtemberg and the remainder of German princes, can lay down their crowns upon the altar of the German fatherland, surely the King of Holland can, and Holland shall, like the Hanse-towns have already commenced to gain by the broadness of the impetus given to commercial progress, the full revival of its ancient renown and cosmopolitan importance as explained already in previous pages.

When, in the rotation of history, the Dutch yielded their supremacy of the commerce of the world to the British, the Americans, although indifferent to the power of the latter, nevertheless always considered the English, in case of aggression, a competent foe to compete with, but never did they estimate Germany or any other nation as of any real consequence in the balance of power of the world. Even France never excelled much in their eyes beyond a continental European power far less than any other power upon the continent of Europe; and that little political respect which America had for France as a cosmopolitan power, during the reign of the first Napoleon, was fully obliterated by the *fiasco* the other Napoleon made in Mexico, doubting the Union of the United States of America. Too exalted to take any notice of his non-Monroeian intentions at the time, and too republican and noble to exult over the defeat of the French in this war with Germany, they were like the English, heartily relieved when French influence suddenly disappeared in a cloud.

In Great Britain the change has been equally great. Justly vexed at the inconsistency of her own Government of having inveigled the nation into an alliance with France, at the time of the Crimean war, instead of having elevated, as was then feasible, tiny but vigorous Prussia, for the same purpose of counteracting the influence of Russia in Turkey, etc., is explained from an over-estimation of French power and general importance ever since the reign of the first Napoleon, the world not having had an opportunity afforded of becoming disabused of it. England now embraces the opportunity of not only remembering the *auld lang syne* of Waterloo, and is naturally at all times sweetly reminded of the welfare of her own daughter, but comprehends the harmony of race and religion.

Vice versa the German politicians who are unfriendly to Great Britain, or worse, defend a monarchical against the American form of government, are always theorists who, in their younger days have not traveled outside of the small continent of Europe; they don't know anything of Great Britain and the United States of America either—as nations; they cannot possibly get at any correct conception of what a *cosmopolitan power* really means, because they have not traveled in what is called "the world" nor even themselves been Hamburg or Bremen merchants, of a world-wide influence, to be able to judge correctly of the power of nations. A voyage to the United States of America, continued to China and India, would facilitate their theoretical knowledge, to be condensed into practical views and enable them to more steadily progress.

PART THE FOURTEENTH.

THE COSMOPOLITAN POWER OF THE UNITED STATES OF AMERICA, GREAT BRITAIN, AND UNITED GERMANY.

History, in viewing and recapitulating the social consequences of this war, at this high period of the world's civilization, above all notes the firm basis which education has so far built in Europe, and upon which liberalism securely rests. That basis is of a firmness which no anti-liberalism can distrust or assail. There is no falling back from the height of knowledge attained; there is no labyrinthian darkness in the mind of man when the external sun of liberty, of humane tolerance, of goodness, and of charitable plenty, pierces the openings in the walls of reason, but very dimly lit up at all times in any one by the artificial light of knowledge of any kind. That such is the case in Europe is now an incontrovertible fact, thanks to liberalism, thanks to its causes—education, thanks to America which influenced its application, thanks to steam and telegraph, by which geographical distances have been annihilated, so as to hourly and ceaselessly promote its spread, and thanks to the pioneers of liberalism and those of commerce, a liberalism cosmopolitanly, materially, and practically aiding it. *The anti-liberal constraint in religious, political, and social matters, is gladly found to abate rapidly.* The concentration of crowns, especially in Germany and Italy, asserts the truthful fact.

The non-interference of Great Britain in this war, another important proof of how liberalism is but synonymous of peace, humanity, tolerance, individual comfort and enlightenment, the fruits of education, gathered from the tree of life, which is ordained to be independent. Great Britain, a non-interferent in this war, while an ally of France, showed most undoubtedly that her people acquiesced in the doctrine of the continuancy for the present of monarchial power, for the same careful reasons which Germany and Italy advance. She could not have sided with France against those convictions, as that would have led to revolution all over Europe. Personal restraint, which is so chronic in Great Britain and Germany, it is to be feared if violently rented, would bring untold misery. The ripe fruit of republicanism will fall off the tree of knowledge, without hindrance, in due time, like any fully ripe garden fruit.

The hatred of some of the French people against foreigners—a sickly glare from the smouldering embers of ambition on the part of their monarchial adherents—after France, to-day, is enjoying the practical blessings of the republican form of government, is another reason why the remainder of the people upon the continent of Europe cannot as yet be republican, nor even venture to disarm, especially considered that the normal condition of society is but now enabled to commence changing for the better. France thus herself in danger, cannot be said to enjoy peace. The humane institutions of the republican form of government, as resting upon peace, are already assailed by those rotating dynastical interests of monarchial aspirants there.

In order to henceforth shield Europe against the eventuality of dynastical wars, Great Britain, Germany, and Italy have to unite to guard the liberalism of Europe, synonymous of progress, as resting upon and developing itself in peace only, until that division of the globe shall be so universally intellectual and strong as to respect it law-abidingly.

America, so favorably isolated by the Atlantic, comprehends the stupendous efforts of enlightened Europe struggling to surely and continually, but gradually, advance Freedom. Upon a piece of territory but as large as half the Occident, and crammed with five times the population of the whole of our division of the globe, it is no easy matter to accomplish. It is not only the desparity of population, but a feudal autocratic power now only waning within the latter half of this century, from which public, mature understanding is alone capable of rescuing Liberty, and of comprehending the vastness of the strides which it costs to accomplish it legitimately. Time, the divine ameliorator of Grief, shall soon roll over this war, and the bright encouragement of Hope, diffusing life, enable nations to henceforth insure their happiness and progress peaceably. Then to disarm will be the order of the day. What happiness and wealth is sacrificed by such a state of suspense and dread of war! What misery entailed upon millions of people by the one word " hate "—war, rivalry in physical force, all of which gladiatorship is centered in the two words " uneducated and bad "—America only can as yet comprehend.

Fed during two centuries as was the former monarchial power of France, by the permanent disunion of Germany and Italy, that nutriment is gone, Europe, the hunting ground for man, "fenced in !" "The watch of the Rhine ! a huntsman, a weather-beaten dead shot, on the look-out !" He shall not keep his eye off France as long as the River Rhine flows upon the earth, nor of Europe until it is republican, and is fit to be so called. Until then it will be difficult for

Europe to disarm. That difficulty rests entirely with society, the normal state of which time only can ameliorate the conventional rigor of, and universal education radically change.

That in consequence of the crammed nature of European population within the small periphery of the territorial size of Europe, and that in consideration of the many heterogeneous national elements adhering to legends of the past, hatred of the present, and revenge for the future, " republicanism in its manhood " is yet far distant, is deplorably clear.

The only hope which shall not stay the deliberate progress of Europe, is that Germany, more intelligent than the rest, becomes doubly as numerically strong as France, instead of as to-day, merely equal to her in strength. She will then be able to relax from the rigor of discipline which alone secured to her her physical preponderance, and bestow her exclusive attention to a radical change in the normal rules of her society. From her compact strength she at present may guard peace, although she cannot initiate disarming; but the full development of her greatness depends upon *the social elevation of the people at large, and the cosmopolitan extension of her commerce.*

The nations of United Europe have, therefore, for the present to continue to maintain the folly of former ignorance, and pay for it. That folly, that incubus, that terrible detriment, consisted on the 1st of September, 1871, in maintaining upon land and seas 5,164,300 soldiers and 512,394 horses, and keep from rust 10,224 pieces of artillery, exclusive of about 800 mitrailleuses—of which ruinous investment Germany alone maintains 18 army corps with 37 divisions of infantry and 10 divisions of cavalry, and 337 batteries, actually supporting 1,152,506 men, and caring for 239,314 horses, and keeping on a war footing 824,990 men, with 95,724 horses and 2,022 pieces of artillery.

The consequences of this war recapitulate in this: Great Britain having allied herself in 1856 with France instead of Prussia, entitles the present Union of Germany, since the defeat of the French in this war, to the Netherlands, which viewed as the remnant of the former great Dutch empire, are as such, consistently and inevitably necessary to now contribute to the formation of an equally vast German empire.

The consummation of this desideratum to be considered peremptory as demanded by duty towards the entire Germanic race, embracing all who are at present alienated under foreign monarchical governments—to the detriment of the expansion of the Union in its great aim and strides of progress: the fitness for self-government and the possibility of contributing greatly towards the humanization of mankind at the present age.

Thus the present regeneration of the Netherlands, the Hanse-towns and Baltic ports to their former greatness centuries ago—the realization of the manifest destiny of the German Union, shall induce Great Britain to morally ally herself with Germany, as strictly demanded by Progress, is facilitated by race and religion, is augmented by similarity of character and strength, is made serviceable to mutual advantage because possible, and is incumbent as a duty which the two nations are destined to fulfill unitedly, peaceable and harmoniously, to the glory of civilization.

As to the English language, it is evident it shall become the language of the civilized world, because the United States of America, absorbing the immigration from all parts of it, absorb likewise the various languages.

THE END.

www.ingramcontent.com/pod-product-compliance
Lightning Source LLC
Chambersburg PA
CBHW030356170426
43202CB00010B/1390